training
PLUS

brian CLEGG

training
PLUS

REVITALIZING your training

**KOGAN
PAGE**

First published in 2000

Kogan Page Limited
120 Pentonville Road
London
N1 9JN
UK

Stylus Publishing Inc.
22883 Quicksilver Drive
Sterling
VA 20166-2012
USA

© Brian Clegg, 2000

British Library Cataloguing in Publication Data

A CIP record for this book is available from the British Library.

ISBN 0 7494 3188 1

Typeset by Jean Cussons Typesetting, Diss, Norfolk
Printed and bound in Great Britain by Clays Ltd, St Ives plc

To Gillian, Chelsea and Rebecca

CONTENTS

PREFACE

The methods and techniques of training are well established. So well established that the tricks of the trade have become hackneyed and tired. We have all been to a session where we've thought 'if we get broken up into groups so we can role play then report back one more time, I'll scream'. At the same time, companies rarely give training the value it deserves. However much you see 'training and development is our highest priority' splashed across the report and accounts, when money gets short, training is one of the first areas to face cuts.

Training+ applies the power of business creativity to training, developing new ways of getting the message across, both to those who pay for training and those who receive it. With full reference to the wide range of opportunities made possible by multimedia and the Web, *Training+* never fails to take into account the impact of technology, but doesn't ignore the most powerful training resource of all – people.

Filled with specifics to try out, *Training+* is a very practical book that follows through the process of training, discovering where it can (and where it should) be taken into a new dimension. It is not intended as a beginner's guide to training, but rather provides a series of incremental steps, taking a training organization or an in-house training department from its present state to a whole new level.

Whether training and development is your business or you are a manager who wants to get the most out of your staff, it's time for *Training+*.

ACKNOWLEDGEMENTS

This book depends on the training experience of a wide range of people. My particular thanks for the helpful contributions of Paul Birch, Rod Murray, Tim Pickles, Julie Reid and Training Zone. At Kogan Page, an accolade to Philip Mudd for making it fun to work with a publisher, and for highlighting the need for something beyond the everyday in training.

ZONE 1
INTRODUCTION

TRAINING – THE GOOD NEWS

There has never been more need for training and education. A hundred
years ago, change was like the slow, steady flow of an untroubled river.
You could start a job at the age of 14 and expect still to be doing it until
you were too old to work. Companies could realistically offer a job for
life to a worker who was happy not to cause any trouble. It's not that
there wasn't change, but the changes that occurred, apart from one-off
catastrophes like the First World War, were manageable and unthreat-
ening.

We have a very different picture now. Change is the norm. Not a
gradual change but a hectic, ever-accelerating explosion of change. No
one expects to stay with the same company for life. Many are opting for
self-employment or being forced into it. Knowledge that was good a year
ago is already becoming out of date. Stability is for wimps. In this frantic
world, training can be both an anchor and a lifeline. An anchor because
it has a clear, focused objective, and a lifeline because it enables the individual to keep up with the pace of change and enables the company to
keep above water. Training has become the number one survival pack for
business.

TRAINING – THE BAD NEWS

So far, so good. If you are a trainer you are probably patting yourself on
the back for being such a valuable person. The truth is that while the
previous section is entirely true, training *can* be all these good things, in
practice it rarely is. Ask anyone who works in a large company to name
the dynamic, important departments in the company. They might

mention marketing or sales. They might come up with some operational functions. They are very unlikely to mention training. Time for some home truths:

1. Many training departments have a bad image.
2. Many companies will say training and development are amongst their top priorities. Almost always they change their mind when money is short. See the mini-case below.
3. Too much training that is currently undertaken has very little impact on what the trainees do when they return to the workplace at the end of the course.
4. Too much training is uninspiring.
5. In a world of change, it's time for a shake-up in training and development.

Bad timing

I recently turned up at meeting with the management development manager of one of the UK's largest corporates. She had asked me to come in to talk about putting together some courses for the company. When I arrived she wasn't available. She had got tied up in an internal meeting. Instead I met with six members of the various training and development sections. They were very interested in what I had to say, but felt it unlikely that we would be able to take our discussions any further.

The reason behind this failure was an object lesson in the realities of training's position in business priorities. The management development manager was in a meeting with her boss, deciding which of the trainers were to lose their jobs and which were to move to a different role. The company was just about to announce its worst financial results in a long time. Rather than recognizing that this showed a desperate need for development, the knee-jerk reaction was to slash the training budget.

The company in the mini-case is generally considered to be an enlightened employer. It talked a lot about people development. It ran company-wide programmes. It had a glossy management academy. But the moment things got tough, it was time to stomp on training.

Now it might seem that I am being a little naïve here. Of course training was going to be cut. Cost-cutting measures were essential for the company's survival. Everyone thinks that their own little bit of the company is the only one that should be preserved intact. No doubt, for instance, the IT department would also be arguing that it shouldn't be cut, because it enabled the company to function more cheaply. But the fact remains that this example illustrates the fragility of senior management's regard for the benefits of training. If they really believed the stuff they said about development, this is the one thing they would ring fence. It's rather as if someone announced that 'our top three priorities are education, education, and education', then as soon as there was a deficit switched to 'cost cutting, cost cutting, and cost cutting'.

I am not arguing that the corporate's approach is correct. I believe that developing staff to their full potential is essential for any company, and that it is doubly required when times are hard. But when looking at the future of training, and how to change the approach we take to people development, it is essential that it is seen in its true light. The real world is rarely like the textbook — or like the company's mission and goals.

BEING MORE CREATIVE

The only hope, both to give training and development a higher profile in a business and to make it more effective, is to be more creative. It is no longer good enough to rely on the way things have always been done, we need to pile new ideas into the training arena. Not just a spot of tweaking, but radical change.

It's all very well to say that there is a need to be more creative about training, but what are you going to do about it? There are a number of options. You can sit and wait for inspiration to strike — but you might be waiting for a very long time. Alternatively, you can scour the world and find the best of what's out there and copy it. This isn't a bad strategy, but you will need to keep up your survey constantly — otherwise you will always remain behind the times.

Learning from other trainers is something we should all be doing (it would be painfully ironic if trainers were not able to learn from others), but it simply isn't enough to copy. A better stance is to take the best of what everyone else is doing and add a little something extra. Best of all, you can ignore what everyone else is doing and come up with something totally new. Then, in the process of making your new idea practical, you can steal lots of good ideas from other people (remember that ideas can't be copyrighted) to improve your own.

This is all very well, but being more creative about training implies being creative in the first place. Many of us reluctantly feel that while we're quite good at getting things done, we are not really creative. That's for the others to do. You only have to listen to advertising agencies talking about 'creatives' – what does that make the rest of us? While it is certainly true that some people are inherently more creative than others, it is also true that we can all increase our individual creativity by large factors. This can be achieved using simple techniques, derived from psychological study of the nature of thought and ideas, decision making and problem solving. This isn't the place for a treatise on the mechanics of becoming more creative. A number of books are listed in the appendix if you would like to find out more. The point is rather that we need to be aware that creativity can be harnessed to help with training.

To get beyond the limits of traditional training we have to be creative about everything in the process. Sometimes this creativity can come from unexpected directions, like facing up to the difference between reality and how things are usually painted. In one of the (otherwise excellent) books I read in preparation for writing *Training+* I came across a list of reasons why managers might want to train their staff personally. The benefits given were 'enhancing topic-specific skills and knowledge, getting the right results, improving leadership skills, and a better understanding of the training environment'. There was no mention of one of the most significant factors on the mind of every manager who decides he or she should lead a training course – it's a cheap option.

According to conventional accounting wisdom, this isn't the case. After all, a manager's salary is higher than that of most trainers. But the real world doesn't work like this. The manager's salary will be paid whether or not the training happens, and whether or not a trainer is brought in. The total drain on the manager's budget is greater if someone else does the training. Okay, another task won't get done, but managers' costs aren't allocated to tasks. So it's a money-saving move for the manager to do the training. Creativity is sometimes about taking the real-world view when everyone else maintains a comfortable fiction. Real people do things for a whole range of reasons. Most real decisions are made more by gut feel than by weighing up objective facts. To gain the creative edge it will sometimes be necessary to have the clarity of vision to see what is really driving your stakeholders.

CREATIVE TRAINING

Creativity applies to training in three different ways. We can be more creative about the way we present training to the company, ensuring that it really is regarded as a business imperative rather than something to be dropped by the wayside as soon as times get hard. We can be creative about the way we train. And we can incorporate the techniques of creativity in the training itself. You will find examples of all three here. As has already been stated, this isn't the place to go into creativity in any depth, but consider a few of the prime tenets of creativity when applied to training:

- **Creativity is limited by our assumptions** – we are all the time making assumptions about what is and what must be. This means that we limit the possible directions we go in for new ideas, and squash many promising ideas because we assume that they are impractical or undesirable – or that they will break some rule. Look out for assumptions when you are considering a session of training. What are you assuming about your trainees and their sponsors? About their needs? About who initiates training? About the environment? About the materials and methods? Be prepared to question all these assumptions.
- **Creativity often involves looking differently at the problem** – have you got the requirement right? How would a totally different person, with different experience, deal with your training requirement? What would a nine-year-old child or a historical character make of it?
- **We don't want to look silly, or get it wrong** – many great ideas never surface, because the individual who thinks of them considers the ideas too silly or worse still that he or she will get something wrong. Most good ideas appear silly early on in their lives, until we have developed them and got them into context. And the only way to succeed creatively is to get things wrong, learn from your mistakes and move on fast. All too often training takes the reverse

view. Negative feedback is considered a criticism to be avoided rather than a desirable thing to make the course even better. That's not creative.

- **Creativity often involves moving totally away from the problem** – don't assume that the only way to develop a computer course is to work with computers, or that the only way to teach computing is with computers. Sometimes it's beneficial to get right away from your problem, then you can work back to it a very different way. Try picking a randomly selected picture from a colour supplement. Note down what it makes you think of. Then look at how these associations could be of use to you in your training. Start elsewhere and move back.

- **Go for appeal and originality first** – it is pretty easy to take a really appealing, original idea that's a little crazy and make it practical. It's much harder to take a totally practical, everyday idea and make it appealing and original. Much harder. Try to come up with new and exciting approaches first, *then* worry about making changes to make things work.

FINDING YOUR WAY AROUND
TRAINING+

This book is structured a little differently from most. Rather than having chapters it is broken into functional zones. The first three zones provide the background to the fourth, which is a collection of actions to move your training from the mundane to *Training+*. The last zone helps you put together an agenda for change.

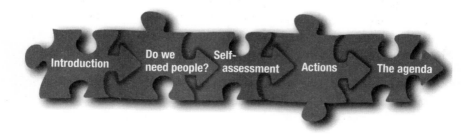

The actions zone itself divides into six sections, each providing practical topics to carry forward and transform your training in everything from development to delivery.

Each section has a wide range of topics giving new directions to consider. As you proceed through the sections you can mix and match the actions you require. The sections start with a key topic – this has been selected to have the maximum impact, to get *Training+* started with a bang. It isn't essential to implement this topic first – in fact, it isn't essential to implement this topic at all – but it will usually provide maximum leverage to get a change under way.

ZONE 2

DO WE NEED PEOPLE?

Before moving into training itself, this zone looks at what the new training delivery mechanisms, from on-the-spot intelligent help to multimedia and the Web, can offer, and whether there needs to be anything else. New technology training will also appear throughout the actions zone.

A NEW WORLD

Training has traditionally been a conservative business. For hundreds of years the biggest step forward was the move from chalk and talk to whiteboard and talk. But like the rest of the world, training has not been able to resist the impact of technology. The communications vehicles available to the trainer have become more sophisticated as we have seen the move from chalkboard to whiteboard to overhead projector to computer projector. The computer has provided direct training through computer-based training (CBT). And there has been a similar revolution in distance learning, with the evolution of the correspondence college into broadcast education and interactive training via the Internet.

It is a reasonable question, given the cheapness (once set up) and 24 hours a day, seven days a week availability of training based on new technology, to wonder whether or not we still need human trainers. Is there any place for people in the training business, outside production and sales of training materials? In fact, there is, but before seeing how, it is worth taking a tour of some of the bigger forces to impact training and to consider their implications for training and *Training+*.

CET

There was a time when computer-based training (CBT) was seen as the great hope for the future. It was cheap to set up and could be undertaken in the trainee's spare time. It had flexibility, being equally at home in a training room and on the desktop. It could even be undertaken at home. Unfortunately, on the whole, pure computer-based training is not very effective. Making use of the full multimedia might of modern computers is too expensive for most niche training vendors, so CBT seems boring when compared with the glossy video and slick interaction of a computer game that can take hundreds of thousands of dollars to produce. The use of media is often closer to a 1950s slide show than the output of a 21st-century TV company. CBT fails to capture the imagination.

CBT is not going to go away, but it is changing. New developments in information technology are helping with this. The digital versatile disc (DVD) allows much more multimedia content to be included in a computer-based course. The Internet provides more flexibility and depth. Natural language and just-in-time training put the CBT where we need it. But the idea of sitting down and working through a course on a standalone PC is on the way out. A more powerful picture is CET – computer enhanced training: combining the best of human training with the support power of the computer, and bringing training elements into aspects of everyday work. CET is here to stay, and will appear in various guises throughout this book.

THE INTERNET

The implications of Internet technology for training have still to be fully absorbed by the training establishment, but the potential is immense. Online learning delivered through this technology (whether openly on the Internet or in-house on an intranet) combines huge flexibility of sourcing with worldwide delivery, and places control very much in the hands of the trainee. Just as the printed page provided a common platform for textbooks, the Internet provides a common hypertext platform for the delivery of training.

Hypertext on hypertext

Hypertext is a term devised by IT visionary Ted Nelson to describe a mechanism for linking blocks of text together. When a piece of hypertext is clicked on with the mouse, a new piece of text expanding on the hypertext or branching off from it is revealed. It could be a definition, it could be a related reference or further reading. Hypertext can be used for anything from footnotes to making the structure of a whole document or book flexible, so that the path through the information is that desired by the reader, rather than that envisaged by the writer.

Brian Clegg, PC Week *article*

As usual with the introduction of a new technology like this, there is a degree of inertia. Inexperienced designers will often attempt to use the new technology as if it were its predecessor. The temptation is, both because it's cheap and because it's easy, simply to push a paper-based training course onto the Internet. But this does not do justice to the power of the medium. Human beings don't think linearly. Our memories and creative processes leap about through a series of links and associations. We also use images and models to process, internalize and recall information. Good use of Web-based training can bring that same strongly linked and image-rich approach. We can put control of the flow and the direction much more into the hands of the trainee than was possible with conventional means.

Internet-based learning has also begun by picking off the 'easy' topics – hard skills, often around IT and the use of software. It will be in the development of soft skill programmes that the Internet will really blossom – but that will require a more creative view of the e-course, making full use of the non-linear and interactive features of the Net.

One key aspect in which the Internet differs from every previous training medium, including computer-based training, is the depth of resources that sit behind an Internet-based course. Trainees can explore a topic further, reaching into resources that the course builder does not have to painstakingly write, relying on the depth of content of the World Wide Web. To go beyond the totally structured course requires greater awareness of how to mine the Internet for information both in the course builder and in the trainee (see Appendix, p 183 for more on Internet mining), but this is a small price to pay for the extra depth and flexibility that comes for free with the Internet.

PROMPTS AND GUIDANCE

One possibility that technology brings into play is just-in-time training. No one likes taking the time to go on a training course when under pressure. As a trainee, training can provide an enjoyable break from real work (no, really – let's be honest), but that is a pleasure you can put off almost indefinitely when the boss is crying out for action. What would be ideal is if we could learn the basic principles, then launch into a real task, with a trainer lurking in the background. If we got stuck, we could call in the trainer to help out; until then we would get on with the job uninterrupted.

Such a just-in-time training technique is nice in theory, but not so good in practice. Even if there were enough trainers around that we could all have one on call during working hours, the cost would be prohibitive. However, this problem doesn't negate the underlying thesis that what the trainee wants to do is get the task completed, not perform the learning for its own sake.

Computer software increasingly has the mechanisms to provide a form of just-in-time training, and as more and more tasks are undertaken via computers, the scope for this form of training grows daily. At its simplest, this involves a form of help system. The trainee is in the middle of a task and realizes that it is not obvious what to do next. For instance, he or she might be writing a letter to everyone in the department. The basics of the letter have been written, but the trainee doesn't know how to merge this text with a set of names and addresses.

Rather than abandon the task until the trainee can attend an appropriate advanced word-processing course, the trainee clicks on the help button and types 'mail merge'. A set of instructions appear on the screen. In the more sophisticated form of this basic approach, the trainee can type a question in English, such as 'How do I merge my letters with addresses?' and be pointed to appropriate assistance.

A second level is not just to give the trainee instructions but to use the interactive nature of the environment to provide CET. Here, in a similar situation, the trainee has typed in a request for help with mail merge. As well as text, the help system comes up with the option 'Show me'. The trainee clicks on this, then watches as the program takes over the computer, moving the mouse cursor around to click on the appropriate menus and buttons until the task is accomplished.

Some processes are sufficiently frequently undertaken that the dividing line between training and support gets fuzzy. This is where the so-called wizard comes in, a step-by-step set of cue cards that not only advise the trainee on what to do next, but provide a framework for action, presenting only those options and controls relevant to the present stage of the process.

We are, by now, used to such prompts and guidance in office software, but they have the potential to be applied to anything from operating machinery to problem determination. Increasingly also, the software that provides help can monitor what is happening and proactively offer assistance, rather than wait to be asked. This is currently present in simple prompts from office software ('You look like you are writing a letter, do you need help?'), but could become much more sophisticated. For example, as speech recognition software improves, it would be possible for a computer to follow a telephone conversation and offer a customer-support agent or sales agent guidance on dealing with the current customer.

In principle these techniques could replace personal expertise. Just as a calculator tends to displace mental arithmetic rather than enhance it, these systems used incorrectly could be seen as a way of displacing human reasoning. However, knowledge is a hybrid of information, the ability to apply that information and the intelligence to adapt and mix factors to deal with a new situation. It is much better for such systems to train up a person, so that the individual has flexible knowledge that can be applied in parallel but in different areas, rather than simply automate a process, leaving the individual unaware of what is going on. The technology doesn't care how it is used – it's up to us. But the fact remains that this technology has the growing opportunity to deliver just-in-time training.

DIY MULTIMEDIA

Traditionally the development of multimedia training materials has been an expensive business that could only realistically be carried out by professional programmers. There were some 'easy' methods of constructing multimedia training, probably best demonstrated in the Asymetrix Toolbook product and Apple's Hypercard, but these remained niche applications. Similarly it was possible to use the hypertext nature of the Windows help system to put together training packages, but the design side of Windows help has always been painfully messy.

The mass-market nature of the World Wide Web has changed all this. There are at least half a dozen powerful packages on the market, priced at the level of domestic software rather than professional design software, that can be used to assemble Web sites and hence multimedia training packages. Bear in mind that the Internet is not needed to make use of Web technology. The principal components are just a browser (freely available, and present on practically every modern PC) and a series of data files using the HTML mark-up language. These files are generated with remarkable ease by products like Microsoft FrontPage and Adobe PageMill. Once produced they can simply be put onto a CD-ROM – there is no need for the Internet. Couple the ease of production with the cheapness of modern CD-ROM writers and the multimedia course is a lot easier to produce than once was the case.

The impressive thing about using a product like FrontPage to put together your own course is how much the package does for you. Throwing in the basic text is no harder than using a word processor, while the package will handle many of the navigation features automatically. There is straightforward support for using graphics (including clickable image maps), sound and video. There is also support for the easily produced animated GIF format that allows simple animated icons and diagrams to be generated. If you have the skills to put together the content and structure of an online course, there is no excuse now for not developing it yourself. At the very least you can have a working prototype to test out the concept and sell it to your management. It may be that you then have it redesigned professionally, or it may be that your product is so good that you want to stick with it. Either way, simple Web site design makes DIY multimedia a very attractive option.

ARE WE DOOMED?

However good all this technology is, the trainer still has a place. Even if all training were provided by computer systems, there would be roles in design and development and in matching the training requirement and delivery. In practice, though, the trainer as a human component of a training session is still invaluable. Whether talking to a large group or working one-on-one, the trainer's flexibility, responsiveness to the trainee's need and ability to generate a human relationship with the trainee are essential.

We shouldn't overlook the value of that relationship. Training is, in essence, a form of communication, and the better the relationship we have with the other people involved, the better that communication. Being taught and helped by a real person feels better than interacting with a computer, however clever and multimedia-rich the application. The human trainer isn't doomed, but needs to take care that his or her USP (unique selling proposition) is always to the fore. If you can excel at flexibility and responsiveness and communication, you can beat a computer hands down. If you are inflexible, cold and poor at communicating, you are allowing your advantage to crumble.

Technology is here to stay in training. It does a lot of good. But the way forward is the integration of human-originated and computer-enhanced training. Seen the right way, the computers aren't a threat, they are an opportunity. Unfortunately, the idea of seeing problems as opportunities has been so overworked that it has become a cliché. It doesn't stop it being true in this case.

BACK TO THE FUTURE

Despite this paean to the wonders of technology, high tech doesn't have to feature in every piece of training. Sometimes it is beneficial to take a step back and do without technology entirely. When the entire world is using video projection and interactive multimedia packages, turning up with a flip chart and some pens can provide an effective contrast. However, there's no way to ignore the impact new technology can have. When developing your training plans, when putting together new courses, you need to be considering how a mix of the new and the best of the old can be used to carry forward training into the realm of *Training+*.

ZONE 3

SELF-ASSESSMENT

The intention of *Training+* is to go beyond the current state of training to make it not just good, but excellent. This self-assessment zone helps readers assess their (and their organization's) current state in each of the six sections of the action zone, providing a guide to balancing the different topics and assessing particular need for activity.

STARTING POINTS

It is worth emphasizing again that *Training+* is not about doing more of the same. But there is still value in being clear just how you currently work, as well as looking for the opportunities to move in a new direction. In this assessment process we are not looking for detail, but the broad direction, the key initiatives and the techniques used to support each of the action sections.

This is not a comprehensive overview of everything you ever needed to know about training. Instead, we are looking at areas where the introduction of some of the *Training+* actions could enhance the effectiveness of your training.

For each section rate your current performance in the key questions below. You can do this either as H (high), M (medium) and L (low) or on a scale out of 10 if you prefer. Each question identifies the actions that might best be used to help in this arena.

ENVIRONMENT

The quality of your training will inevitably be influenced by the environment in which you do that training. The training environment is something that seems to be considered in waves. Sometimes it is given a lot of importance, sometimes it is pushed to one side as incidental to the main function of training. These questions will help examine your approach to the training environment:

- How good are you at being flexible in timing and location of training?
  (*Let's do lunch*, page 23; *Progressive seminars*, page 25)
- How much are you prepared to put effort into ensuring that the training environment is stimulating and different?
  (*The exotic*, page 27; *Themed events*, page 30; *Housebound*, page 43)
- How much are you prepared to vary your training based on the environment that is made available?
  (*Using what's around*, page 33; *Using a hellhole*, page 47)
- How well do you understand the potential of the Internet as a training environment?
  (*Web training*, page 36)

COMMUNICATION

Communication is at the heart of training. Whether indirect or direct, all training, all learning involves some form of communication. Sometimes it is an aspect of communication that breaks down and leaves our training stranded high and dry. It has to be a priority:

- Do your trainees come out of your training sessions with a buzz?
  (*Energy transfer*, page 50; *Giving it all you've got*, page 63; *Bite-sized chunks*, page 71)
- Do your materials give the training a real lift?
  (*Slides that scintillate*, page 53; *Hollywood or bust*, page 60; *Props*, page 73)

- Are your personal communication skills impressive?
  (*Speaking to the masses*, page 58; *Non-verbals*, page 68)
- Is the trainer/trainee relationship right for the most effective training?
  (*Bonding*, page 76; *Manager as trainer*, page 78)

VEHICLES

The method that is used to put across the training can make all the difference to the impact on the trainees. If I had to pick a single topic that I think has most mileage of all the sections, it's the key topic in this area. The distinction between environment, communication and vehicles is to some extent arbitrary – don't worry too much about the labels, just look at what you are doing and what you need:

- How much can the trainees determine the content of their own training?
  (*Target plus toolkit*, page 82; *Action learning*, page 109)
- Do you have ways that trainees can effectively run their training themselves in any environment?
  (*Books alone*, page 91; *The humble cassette*, page 95)
- How much do you explore the training legacy of childhood?
  (*Playing games*, page 87; *I want to tell you a story*, page 97)
- How much do you bring the unexpected into your training?
  (*Role play revisited*, page 100; *Breakout groups overhauled*, page 105; *Surprise packages*, page 111)

SUPPORT

The training session alone can only go so far. If training is to be really effective there need to be ways that the training is carried back into the workplace or normal life. Putting enough effort into such support is where much training falls down, yet however brilliant the course, unless the training is used, it is a waste of time and money:

- How much do you use books and software to extend your training?
  (*Books*, page 115; *Software*, page 136)

- How much do you use electronic means to extend your training?
  (*E-mail extensions*, page 118; *Intranet reinforcement*, page 121)
- How much do you use prizes and giveaways to reinforce the message and make learning fun?
  (*Prizes*, page 123; *Giveaways*, page 127)
- How much do you support your training by manipulating mood and making use of what you can find?
  (*Warm-ups*, page 130; *Spur of the moment*, page 133)

DEVELOPMENT

Your training is only as good as the quality of your training development, and even the best of training will date quickly, especially in high-technology areas. Being flexible and constantly evolving your courses will make your training future-proof:

- How formally do you make sure that your training development is creative?
  (*Creativity techniques*, page 140)
- How flexible are you about changing the content of your course?
  (*Flexible development*, page 146; *Fun feedback*, page 151)
- How good at you at finding new content and materials?
  (*Finding your materials*, page 143)
- How much do you look outside the world of training for ideas?
  (*Ideas – stealing and creating*, page 148)
- How well do you monitor the impact of your training?
  (*Evaluating benefit*, page 155)

TARGETING AND MARKETING

The drivers we are looking for here are those that are important to your training and learning endeavours as a business. If you work in an in-house training department, think of what you would need to do if you were to take your part of the department and spin it off as a separate company. If you work for an independent training company (but aren't already the boss), think about what you would do if the managing director asked you to take over the company tomorrow:

- How well do you match training to individuals' needs?
  (*Matching the individual*, page 159; *Wants vs needs*, page 162)
- How well do you do at making the appropriate people aware of your training and getting them onto the courses?
  (*Invitations and advertising*, page 168)
- How well do you market the training department/your company?
  (*Selling training benefits*, page 164, *Improving an in-house training department's visibility*, page 174)
- How much business training and experience do your trainers have?
  (*Make trainers business people*, page 172)

A BALANCE

In taking action to change and enhance your training the aim is to achieve a balance: to keep the best of your current approach to training, but to embrace the benefits that *Training+* can bring. It may be that in some areas there is nothing to be done. That's fine. When you have seen the available actions in the next zone, you will have the opportunity to develop an agenda for change. The important thing is to ensure that you enhance the areas you have identified as having weaknesses by using the relevant *Training+* actions.

But don't plunge into the decision yet. The placement of the actions zone between the assessment and the agenda is not accidental. Just seeing the range of actions available will (and should) influence your agenda. With your requirements in mind, browse through the actions zone before building that agenda.

ZONE 4
ACTIONS

This is a book that is primarily about action. Not in the formal sense of action learning (see page 109), but the requirement to take action to move your training on to a new state of effectiveness. This zone contains a wide range of topics covering actions, divided into six major sections.

THE ACTION SECTIONS

First comes the *Environment* – influencing the quality of training through the location and context of the session. *Communication* covers the central nature of training. It involves a two-way communication between trainer and trained, and this section considers the best approaches to communication. From there we move on to the *Vehicles*, the tools and techniques of training beyond the generics of communication. The fourth section, *Support*, provides an insight into the best ways to extend the training back into the workplace and support the training effort to get maximum effect. Next is *Development*, looking at the use of feedback and the continuous development of content to ensure the best fit to the training need. Finally, in *Targeting and marketing*, the focus is on training as a business. It covers the need to justify your training, get a good fit to your requirement, keep training cost-effective and sell it to those who are to be trained. It might seem strange that this section comes last – it is done intentionally to show the cyclical nature of the sections. It could equally have appeared at the beginning or before development. The important thing is that all six sections of the actions zone are considered.

If you need guidance in selecting topics that will be of most benefit, consider your current state from the Self-assessment zone. Look for gaps in your current state. Otherwise you might find it effective to skim through the action topics, dipping in where an introduction sparks your interest. Sometimes it isn't the most obvious, planned change that makes all the difference, but something you spot by chance. You will then have a chance to revisit the actions in the Agenda zone.

4A ENVIRONMENT

We all have stereotyped views of a training location. It might be a large hall for a lecture-style session, a room full of PCs for technical training or a horseshoe of tables with breakout rooms for management training. This section looks at the failings of traditional locations. It examines the opportunities for using a whole range of environments from a domestic house to an airliner – and ways of bringing conventional locations alive.

A fundamental assumption of much training is that the individual comes to the training, rather than the training to the individual. This is partly for cost reasons, and partly because self-managed training is often a poor second best. The individual also misses out on much of the benefit of interaction with other trainees. Some of the *Environment* sections look at ways that new technology and a new approach to people can transform bringing training to the individual.

Sometimes the division between this and subsequent sections is fuzzy. When dealing with training on the Web, for instance, the environment effectively becomes the delivery vehicle – and the means of communication as well. Yet environment has a strong enough influence on the quality of training to be considered in its own right.

Key topic – Let's do lunch

If we are realistic, we have to recognize that however many fancy statements appear in the annual report, training is never going to be given the on-the-day importance it deserves. Taking important staff or managers offline for training will always be resisted by their bosses. Increasingly we have to look for alternatives to training in working hours.

Food for thought

A large company had provided all its managers with access to the Internet from their desktops, but was rather embarrassed to discover that this powerful resource wasn't being used. After briefly playing with the World Wide Web, most managers were finding that they could get little business value from the Internet and didn't return to it.

The training department set up half-day sessions on using Web browsers and finding information, but there was very little take-up. It was hard to justify time spent in training on a subject for which the need was not clearly felt. Some while later, the training department tried brief lunchtime sessions combined with giving away a book on the subject (*Mining the Internet* – see the appendix, page 183). The result was a total turn round. It became one of the most popular sessions the department had run.

It's not hard to see why a lunchtime session plus a book was more effective than a half day of training in this example. The principle behind getting the most out of the Internet can be put across quickly and simply, while getting a deeper understanding of the skills is best done while actually using a computer with a guide at your side.

While this quick introduction approach isn't suited to all topics, a surprising range of subjects can be covered as long as the session is accompanied by appropriate support material. The lunchtime period is an attractive target. Putting training before or after work eats into precious home time. Having it during working hours takes key workers away from the task. But lunchtime has its drawbacks too.

Not taking people out of work makes a statement about the importance of this training. It says that the company isn't prepared to give time to it, so it can't be all that valuable. This message has to be countered by making sure it is clear that the approach is being taken as the best of both worlds. It also has the potential to irritate the staff, eating into 'their' time and disrupting an opportunity to refresh their batteries for the afternoon's work.

To overcome the reaction that it is taking up 'their' time, the session needs to be made as attractive as possible. After all, no one complains about attending social clubs or undertaking sports activities in the lunch break. A combination of good advertising, an entertaining approach and clear personal benefits should make a lunchtime session an attractive activity in its own right. There should be no stigma attached to not attending. And the lack of time for recovery should be countered by providing lunch, a comfortable environment and a topic that is well removed from everyday work. A course on 'filling in form 35b' or 'procedures for purchasing paper clips' is not a good lunchtime topic.

Given this approach, the lunchtime session is a great opportunity. Making it attractive should include a giveaway (see *Giveaways*, page 127), perhaps in the form of a book (see *Books*, page 115). Probably the most important advice is not to try to cram too much into the session. Realistically you have three-quarters of an hour at most. Trying to force a whole morning's training into this time will just give slides full of text and no time to think. The best approach is either to split a subject across several lunchtimes (if you do this, consider repeat sessions in case one is missed, and avoid school holidays), or to have a very tightly scripted introductory session, then send attendees away with follow-up material like a book, Web site or CD-ROM that can be used to expand on the subject as and when the trainee feels is appropriate.

If the lunchtime approach is really to take off it is best to have a regular slot, so potential trainees can be used to keeping Tuesdays free because that's lunchtime seminar day. However, the content of such a slot should vary greatly from week to week. Sameness is the constant risk arising from a regular schedule – there's a need to inject variety to keep the process interesting. With these provisos in mind, the lunchtime session has the potential to be the vehicle for getting life back into your training.

Progressive seminars

There's a form of social meal popular in some areas called the progressive supper. A group gets together and has the starter of a meal at one house. They then all walk on to a second house for the main course. Another location provides the pudding, and perhaps another still the coffees. It splits the load, gives more variety of catering and adds spice to the whole event. There's a lesson for training here.

La croyance au progrès est une doctrine de paresseux, une doctrine de Belges. C'est l'individu qui compte sur ses voisins pour faire sa besogne.

[Belief in progress is a doctrine of idlers, a doctrine for Belgians. It is the individual relying on his neighbours to do his job.]

Charles Baudelaire

Baudelaire was unnecessarily hard on progress (and probably on Belgians too). In fact, in looking for a suitable quotation to start this topic it's surprising how often progress gets a raw deal. The trouble is politicians and others in power are overly fond of using progress as an excuse to trample all over the concerns and considerations of others. That's not what this particular bit of progress is about – instead we are returning to an earlier meaning of the word, when an important person's progress was their formal travel from place to place.

Most training suffers from being static. There's something about being stuck in a training room on a two-day course that totally drains the enthusiasm by the middle of the second day. In normal life, unless we are asleep, we don't usually spend more than a couple of hours in the same place doing the same thing. Assuming the intention isn't to put the trainees to sleep, breaking up a course that lasts more than half a day is a good move.

There are a number of features of a progressive supper that can be beneficial to training. The load is split between a number of cooks – generally training will benefit from not staying with the same trainer through a whole day or longer. Give them some variety of tone, delivery and viewpoint. In the progressive supper you get to eat your food in a range of different environments. Just doing different parts of the training in different locations can give it a boost (see *Housebound*, page 43 for a very specific example of this).

One of the most important factors in the success of the progressive supper is the walking between venues. It's not unusual for the walks to last 10 to 20 minutes. This in itself is a model that training could latch on to with significant benefits. Taking the course on a walk between sessions (especially if there's a goal like the location of the next session) can do a lot for a group. There's the physical exercise, getting the blood pumping and life back into listless trainees. There's the move out of the deadening air-conditioned atmosphere. There's the stimulation of new surroundings. And there's the opportunity for much less formal social interaction than when seated in a training room.

Whether the elements of the progressive supper are taken in total or mixed and matched to the requirement, there is a powerful resource here to help with training. As an exercise in creative thinking about training, look at other forms of social gathering. What lessons have they got for a training environment? Spend five minutes thinking about it.

Although it wasn't the intention, you could take the idea to the extreme and have training which is itself mobile. See *The exotic* (page 27) below for some possibilities on mobile training. Here we won't worry too much about what the form of mobility is, but the potential benefits. There is a constantly changing stimulation when attention is flagging. You can move your training venue to a number of sites relevant to the training. In the summer you might even take a training bus to a pick-your-own farm and have a pick-and-eat lunch. Or drop off at a chocolate factory. Perhaps being Belgian isn't so bad after all!

The exotic

To learn well, a group of trainees have to be interested, engaged and full of energy. There are few places less likely to get trainees into this state of mind than a typical training room. Consider the possibilities of the exotic location.

How not to do it

All too often the best examples are of failure. Here's how not to use an exotic location. I once attended a conference and training session at a theme park. It was during the winter, so the theme park was closed to normal visitors. It seemed a wonderful opportunity – we had a theme park all to ourselves. And we would get some training in too.

We turned up at the park on a cold but crisp winter day. The programme looked interesting. It was going to be a great three days. And then we discovered what the course organizers had not bothered to tell us. The theme park wasn't just closed to the public – the rides weren't running at all. We spent three days corralled away from the interesting bits, able to see the rides but unable to go on them. The event did not go well. The exotic is great to add zest to a training session – but to promise the exotic and deliver a cold building site is not a good move.

What is the point of a training location, after all? It's to get the trainees away from the distractions of their everyday work. To get them motivated and energized. And to help them think in new ways. Let's dispose first of the concern that's occasionally raised about exotic locations – all we are doing is replacing one distraction with another (the location).

There is an element of truth here, but only in the case of a short event. It is probably best to keep the exotic for half days or longer sessions. There will be a brief period of distraction initially, but that will soon disperse. What will linger is the location's ability to give extra zest to the training, to provide opportunities for the trainer to do things in a different and more stimulating way. Given an exotic location it may also be appropriate to have a themed event (see the next topic), but it is not essential. Even a straightforward seminar can have more impact in an exotic location.

The exact nature of the location is down to your budget, what is available and how much effort you are prepared to put into the event. They can be as wild and different as you like, or perhaps just a little different, provided you can accommodate your trainees comfortably and safely and the environment doesn't get in the way of the training too much. Here are some example locations. It's anything but exclusive – the list could have continued indefinitely:

- an aircraft, train, bus or liner;
- a theme park;
- a swimming pool;
- a Turkish bath;
- a farm;
- a country house, sea fort or castle;
- at the top of a very high tower;
- a church;
- a lighthouse;
- a safari park;
- a tree house;
- an underground cavern.

The transport examples may be more cramped than a conventional training room, but make up for this in interest. Whether the vehicle actually moves or not is up to you. I've been on a very effective session on a grounded aircraft in a museum – on the other hand, one conference company has a great success with sessions on liners, which take their captive audiences out to anchor in calm waters for the duration of the event. Liners are ideal for large, flexible training sessions, perhaps for a whole department or company. A train, on the other hand, can be more compact, but still have lots of appeal, especially if it's a steam train on a preserved line or a glamorous train like the Orient Express.

Theme parks, as the example shows, can be disappointing if used out of season, but many offer training rooms, and there's a special atmosphere of excitement about the location. A Turkish baths, on the other hand, might not have a training suite, but it's an ideal environment to combine learning with stress reduction – and perhaps team building too. You will have to be careful with the design of your materials if you are not to end up with soggy masses of paper, but the potential is there.

It's not necessary to go through each example in detail. The opportunity is clear. One of the biggest problems conventional training faces is that it is in a rut. A trainee who is new to the training process might find a conventional, hotel-based session with breakout rooms and role play exciting and novel, but when you've done it 10 times the thrill palls. An exotic location can bring the spice back into the training experience, just as an exotic holiday location can spice up a relationship.

Themed events

Giving a training event a theme (other than the task in hand) can help pull together diverse threads and make the whole event more exciting, memorable and effective.

Breaking the rules

In this example the themed event was an idea generation session rather than pure training. Up to now themes have been used much more often in such creativity sessions, but they have equal applicability to training.

'The theme of the event was breaking the rules and so a large part of the day was concerned with those habitually outside the rules in society. Burglars figured large in this. Part of the time the participants dressed in striped T-shirts and black masks and took a bag marked 'swag' out into the hotel to steal something to bring back (used in a creativity technique called *Found object* – see page 33). The theft element and the absurdity of the costume meant that they went a lot further than any other group that I've used *Found object* with. One pair stole an entire set of wrought iron patio furniture and brought it all back into the meeting room. One person stole a bike that was chained to a disused gate so they stole the gate (it lifted off its hinges) as well. One person stole the pay phone from the lobby. One pair was chased from the kitchens by an irate chef when they tried to steal a set of kitchen knives. The creative idea generation session that followed was one of the best I've ever participated in because of the energy and adrenaline that the exercise generated.

'Other events during the day involved the invention of new ball games and ways of misinterpreting the rules that another group had invented. These sessions were interspersed with idea sessions using the rules and rule breaking as stimuli. We also had sessions on what are the rules that exist at work – especially the taken for granted, implicit ones. For example, what are the rules that exist in a hotel, and so on. We then worked on ways of breaking those rules.

'The objective of the day was to generate new product ideas

that broke the rules of the industry. Their measure of success was that they had at least one new product idea by the end of the day. We were hugely successful and they went away with over 20 immediately workable ideas.'

There is something inside us that reacts well to a theme. Our whole mechanism for dealing with the world depends on pattern building. I might not have seen a specific small roundish thing that hops around with a red front and a beak before, but I recognize that it fits within my personal classification of a bird, and specifically a robin. A theme plays to this urge to categorize and build patterns, just as coordinated furnishings do. It can also act as a stimulus to creativity, especially if the theme is divorced from the training requirement and the business.

You can increase the benefit of a themed event by using an exotic location (see above), but that isn't essential. Good themed events can be run anywhere, provided the location is flexible enough to cope with the onslaught – and that's what a good themed event is liable to be, so make sure there are no neighbours to upset.

Having a theme makes it easier to design the course, because you have a central core concept to build your training activities around. The theme provides a constant mental hook that both lets you link back to the event's purpose in a work context, and acts as a constant stimulus for ideas, suggesting new approaches that can be used in the event.

To work well, a themed event should take the theme as far as possible. On one occasion, where the event was about attracting new customers, the theme used was seduction. This session had no seats, only large floor cushions. There was soft lighting, romantic music, fine wine, bowls of fruit, sweets and condoms. (This last was a humorous extension of the theme – as far as we are aware they were only used as balloons.) It's important also that the theme pervades the session. It shouldn't be laid on as a thin veneer, just visible at the start and end – every part of the session should link back to the theme.

It helps with such an approach if you gradually stretch the limits of the trainees, slowly making the impact of the theme more outrageous as the event progresses. Throw them in at the deep end at the start and you may get rebellion. Bring the power of the theme up gradually and it will be accepted (this means that realistically a themed event should be at least a day long). The location for the training should be seen as a set, as if it were taking place on stage or about to be filmed. It should no longer be considered a training room or a hotel suite. Considerable effort needs to be put into the design of the set and how it fits with the course. Allow plenty of time for construction before the event.

A themed event is not a lightweight option. There is a lot of preparation involved, and the trainers have to take on a higher level of risk than normal, because just as in a stage play, the audience must suspend their disbelief and start to take part. If successful, however, you will have reached a level of communication with and input from your trainees that is very rarely achieved. Themed events are much more common in idea generation than training at the moment – this is an opportunity to steal a great idea from elsewhere and to bring it to bear on training.

Using what's around

Ideally, every training event should take place in the perfect location, specially designed to match the requirements of the course. Realistically, life isn't going to be like that. With flexibility, the spontaneous use of what is available can make more than the best of a bad job.

Found objects

In the creativity technique 'found objects' used regularly in my company's creativity training, specific use is made of the surroundings of the course. Many creativity techniques use an item (like a randomly selected picture or word) to start the trainee thinking in new directions, looking at a problem in a different way. In found objects, teams are sent out of the training room as individuals. Each person has to come back with an object. They will then have to explain to the others why it is the most exciting, fascinating thing in their life. There is usually a small prize for the most interesting things brought back.

We have used this technique in a wide variety of locations, some formal, some less so, and the participants never fail to return with something interesting, something to bring a smile. Nothing has been planted beforehand, yet in perfectly ordinary office locations we have had people return with pictures unscrewed from the wall, beer crates, eight-foot-high plants and much more. If you have the incentive, practically any surroundings can provide inspiration and can help your session.

You've got a training event due the following week. The venue is all arranged. Everything was going neatly to plan – only there has been a gas leak and the building is closed. The seminar has to go ahead, but you will need to find a new location. It sounds a disaster, but for once a problem really can be turned into an opportunity. Don't panic; make something of it.

See what is available. Don't limit yourself to the obvious choice of training rooms. (Chances are at this late date all the decent ones will be gone and you'll be left with a hellhole. See *Using a hellhole*, page 47 if you are left with no choice about this.) You might find a large disused office, or even better a whole floor of an open plan office building currently vacant. You might hire a marquee. You might use an aircraft hangar or a vacant factory building or a barn if there's one on your site. (You could also find one off your site, but that's more the subject of *The exotic* on page 27.) Look around for something that will give an edge to the session.

Adopting a strange location will require extra preparation. You will need to check on insurance and fire regulations. You will need to make sure that the location has appropriate fixtures and fittings. Note that appropriate is not the same as 'the usual'. In a barn location, for instance, bales of straw could stand in for seating, safety regulations permitting. However, if the session really does have to go ahead it will be worth undertaking the extra effort – and the sheer novelty of the surroundings will add extra benefit to the training.

In fact this ability to make use of what's around extends far beyond the basic training location. A couple of days before the session, have a wander round. Make a note of anything about the location that is special. Is there some feature of the building that stands out? Is there something outside your training room, or even outside the building that could be useful? Don't be selective, jot down anything that might catch the attention of a five-year-old. (A five-year-old, because they notice so many more things we ignore because we think of them as ordinary.)

Armed with your list, look for opportunities to build what you have noticed into your session, or even rebuild the session around what is there. We once ran a session in a training room that had an open terrace on the roof above it. This free facility just had to be worked into the session – we had the trainees go up to the roof terrace as part of one of the exercises. The novelty (and in this case the fresh air) all helped to keep the training session alive and vibrant.

Every venue is different. Just as an example, we recently used a large open-plan office area. It had been vacated several months before, leaving a wasteland of desks. A foraging expedition the week before came up with a whole host of resources: the desks themselves; various stationery items that had been left behind; posters and notices on the wall; dead and dying plants; a thermometer, stuck on one of the windows behind the venetian blinds; the blinds themselves; push-button security code locks on the doors leading into the office area; moveable screens; a PC monitor with no PC; a handful of telephones; hundreds of telephone sockets; a box containing a pile of old in-house magazines; carpet tiles;

large signs hanging from the ceiling saying what a particular section of the open plan was called; a seat cushion. And so it went on – a treasure trove of possibilities.

It's then just a matter of seeing how the resources might fit in with the session you intend to run. With plenty of imagination almost anything can become a prop in your event. Try it out yourself, now. Have a look round the location you are in at the moment. Look inside and out. Look for small things and large. Make a list of potential resources for a hypo-thetical course. Don't worry about what you will do with them, just make a list of what there is. You'll probably be surprised at the variety of resources available.

In the example above, the need to use what was around was mostly forced, but there is no reason why you shouldn't make use of it to spice up conventional training. You wouldn't want a make-do location every time, but if interest is flagging it can make all the difference. And if you are flexible enough you can always make use of the unique elements in and around your training venue to make it more than an off-the-shelf, everyday session.

Web training

There has never been an information source like the World Wide Web before. It brings a vast array of resources into place behind any Web-based training. The secret of using the Web for training is to leverage this remarkable library.

Web as library

Of course, some would dispute this 'library' label. Whether or not you accept it, depends on your definition of a library. Admittedly the Web is neither comprehensive nor organised, but it is certainly rich in content. I would argue that it is a library, but one that differs widely from the conventional image. This library has huge open windows. All the time writers, businesses and advertisers hurl contributions through the windows to land anywhere. Meanwhile, semi-intelligent robots bustle around, trying to see what's where, clever spiders build webs to link related contributions and an army of mice nibble documents into extinction. It's a library, Jim, but not as we know it.

Brian Clegg, from an article in Professional Manager *magazine*

Developing a Web-based course, whether for the Internet or an intranet, isn't really the subject of *Training+*. Development will be based on a combination of conventional course design and Web design. The main concern for *Training+* is making use of the fact that the Web is not just a delivery mechanism for your course, but far more. We'll come back to that in a moment, but there are other concerns to be addressed. Most important is not to take a course from a different medium and assume you can just churn it out as a Web course.

The core feature of the Web is hypertext. Instead of being a linear document like a book or a training booklet, a Web site consists of small chunks of text tied together by a skein of hot links. Simply pumping text into the Web format defeats the object. You can use the interactive nature of the Web to allow the trainee to select asides and amplifications, to see an overview and then expand where required, to choose the flow through the material and even to take tests. Giving training through the Web without making use of all these is defeating the object.

A second consideration when putting a course onto the Web is designing for your environment. Although in-house intranets and the true Internet use the same technology, your trainees are liable to use quite different mechanisms for accessing them. Where it might be acceptable to put large images and slow-to-load add-ins on the corporate intranet, it's not a good move if the trainee may be accessing the site through a slow modem. Use graphics, certainly – putting together text-only Web training is perverse (though you might like to have a text-only option for those with special accessibility needs), but the graphics need to be snappy and quick to load, put together in such a way that you can get going before the graphics have finished appearing. The trainee should be setting the pace of training, not the download time of your pictures.

But let's return to the fact that the Web is more than a delivery mechanism for your course. Consider the quote above. Libraries are a great place to learn, because there is so much reading beyond the basics of your course manual – but at the same time they are a pain because you have to keep quiet, and work their way. The Web gives you a chance to add a library to your course, yet leave the trainees able to access it where and when they like.

There are three levels at which a library can be bolted onto your course. They aren't exclusive – you can go for all three if you like. Firstly, you can establish your own information archives, specific to your course. If, for example, your students are expected to perform some sort of exercise as part of the course, you can make sure that all the background information they need is available to look up in Web format. Ideally it should be as part of a wider set of information for all your courses, as all trainees can benefit from some experience in tracking down information.

Secondly, you can give the trainees an outbound reference section. This would contain a set of pointers, not to your own sources of information but for information out on the Web. Setting these pointers up requires some time and effort, but it is well worth it. Whether you want to find case studies or facts, background information or practical exercises, the chances are that there is something out there on the Web. With quick references to these sources as the trainee passes through the course, and an external links section so links can easily be revisited, trainees can come back and pull in extra resources whenever they need them.

Finally, the trainees can (and should) be given open access to search the Web themselves. You won't find everything that's relevant if you set up an outbound reference section. In fact, the chances are you won't find 10 per cent of the relevant material, and what you have found will date more rapidly than the course itself. By giving the trainees quick access to Web search engines, and pointers on using them effectively, you can improve their chances of getting real value out of the Web. If using the Web isn't a particular expertise of yours or your trainees, see *Mining the Internet* in the Appendix (page 183).

Using the Web isn't plain sailing, and it's quite possible you've got doubts. Here are the main ones addressed.

They will waste time

Giving employees access to the Web brings out the worst in many employers. We might trust these people with vast quantities of the company's money, but as soon as we let them get to the Web we are convinced they are going to turn into porn fiends and spend all their time aimlessly surfing the Net in search of cheap thrills. Apart from the unfortunate comment this makes on staff relationships, the fact is that the problem is overstated. Everyone will do a little random surfing – but that's part of the point of the Web. It allows new connections and thoughts to be brought into the process. But for most of us, after a quick skim around we are happy to settle back to the task in hand. By all means expect results out of people with access to the Web, but don't fence them in and worry about their abusing your trust.

Web sources might be wrong

It's an apparently worrying fact that Web sources might be wrong. But then, who gets it right every time? Newspapers aren't exactly noted for their error-free reporting. In a recent piece of research I did using a series of books by well-known writers I was given dates of birth for a key individual that varied by a hundred years, and found another important figure, in fact Greek, described as an Egyptian in a book from a very respectable publisher.

Where the Web differs from other forms of publishing is that there is no editorial control. This can be helpful, as it means lots of information that would be excluded from a printed text can be crammed in, but it does mean you have to be more careful about your sources and exactly what is being said. Even so, the Web makes a great source of information. After all, if you're the world's greatest expert on selling paperclips, the chances are you aren't going to write a book and you aren't going to have a *Wall Street Journal* article written about you. However, as an enthusiast (and you have to be an enthusiast to be the world's greatest expert on selling paperclips) you may well have your own Web site and will be able to pass on that expertise to a grateful audience. Now multiply that up by a few million experts and you start to see the benefit of the Web. Of course you've got to be careful, and your Web research pointers should give some assistance on checking the veracity of the information gathered, but the fact that some information on the Web is biased or downright wrong is no reason for not using the Internet effectively.

There won't be anything about our subject

Sometimes this is perfectly true. There are still immense gaps in the knowledge represented on the Web – it's only natural. However, it is astounding just how much information is out there if you go about finding it the right way. Bear in mind too that your trainees may approach that searching in a different way. The chances are that some of them will be able to find information that you can't. Don't assume it isn't there because you can't find it – just warn the trainees that they won't necessarily be able to track down everything.

We don't have the expertise

This isn't excusable. Any training department worth its salt ought to have expertise in finding information on the Web. If not, you are in dire need of training yourselves. You might not be able to build the training Web site itself – that can be left to a third party, but you should be able to identify Web-based resources to help your trainees.

They don't have the expertise

This, too, isn't good, though it's more likely. If there is any danger that your trainees aren't familiar with using the Web for finding business information, there should be an opportunity to find this out early on in the course and do something about it. Ideally using the Web should be as natural to them as using a word processor or pen and paper. You probably don't need to give a full-scale course, though a short lunchtime session is worth considering. In either case, provide copies of a book like *Mining the Internet* (see page 183) to dip into when the trainee hits problems.

We can't link our training site to the Web

Once more inexcusable, this time a problem for which you don't have to take the flak. If your IT department says this isn't possible, hire some new IT people. If they say it's not desirable, make it clear that it is your job to assess desirability and this will be a key part of your training delivery vehicle. It is quite possible that it won't be practical in a day or two, but if it can't be done with a month's warning you should take this as a signal that the IT people don't take the Web seriously and push hard to get things (or them) changed.

Showcase

It's all too easy to get into the habit of thinking that training is one type of process. This topic looks at using a popular information dispersal format that also has the potential for training – the trade fair or show.

Fair's fair

When I ran the Emerging Technology group of a large company we put on a fair, showing the latest developments in IT both within the company and in the outside world. We particularly focused on new directions. The fair proved a great success, attended by a huge range of people from directors to shop-floor workers. We quickly discovered that the borderline between informing and educating is wafer thin. Not only were we making people aware of possibilities, some were staying longer on stalls and getting into the practicalities of the topic – there was no doubt about it, they were learning.

A lesson trainers are often loathe to learn is that there's a lot you can borrow or steal from other professions (see *Ideas – stealing and creating,* page 148, for more on this). There's nothing unique about trainers in this regard. It's a universal shortcoming. We all know that we are the experts in our field (whatever it happens to be) and no outsider is going to come in and tell us what to do. However, to avoid the outside world is crazy, because there are so many opportunities to learn from elsewhere. One vehicle that is worth stealing is the trade show or fair.

We've all been to this sort of thing. There are booths in which a group of people are energetically selling their products to anyone who cares to listen. There are demonstrations and giveaways and leaflets and activity – lots of activity. In fact such fairs have two potential applications for training. The lesser one is as a sales and marketing tool. Try having a training fair, showing just what the training department or company can offer. Have different booths for different courses and subjects and sell just as if you were selling the widgets you made. I've labelled it a lesser approach, but as an activity every year or two to draw attention to your training portfolio it's not a bad scheme, and doubly so if you can tie it in with a captive audience. For instance, if your company has a management conference, having a management training fair at the conference will hugely increase the numbers of managers you get through it.

The more radical use of the concept is for training itself. Consider a fair where each stand deals with a small element of training in one subject. For instance, imagine a time management fair. Some stands could cover time management systems and software. Another might deal with assessing your personal goals. Others could cover handling meetings or coping with e-mail and the phone. Attendees would have a menu card, enabling them to check off the segments of the training they have dealt with. They could browse around, giving as much or as little time as they liked to different aspects of the topic.

Alternatively, you could have a multi-topic fair. For instance, you might have a new management skills fair. One stand could cover creativity. Another might deal with NLP or knowledge management. At such an event, the attendees may well take a more mix-and-match approach, and the tendency would be to give an overview of several topics rather than in-depth learning. But the opportunity would be there to give trainees the chance to pursue topics they wanted more depth in at a later date.

Such an approach puts a different strain on your resources. Instead of needing one trainer (say) for half a day each week for a year, you might need 10 trainers solidly for two days. However, there is also an opportunity to get external support. Supplier companies may be more likely to sponsor a fair than a simple training course. Some stands could be run directly by vendors – for instance in the time management example above, system and software vendors would jump at the chance to be represented. And a business bookshop or publisher can be encouraged to have a stall, giving them sales and helping trainees to expand their business library.

A training fair is not something you can do very often. It takes a lot of organizing and requires a large amount of space and plenty of people. But as an infrequent event both to boost the visibility of your training department or company and to make a real attack on a particular topic, it's a cast-iron Training+ opportunity.

Housebound

We've looked in other topics at the use of different buildings and exotic locations. There is one location that can be very effective, is very widely available and can be surprisingly low cost – a house.

Down in the country

This consultant got remarkable results from the use of a house.

'This was a team-building event for a small group (six people) who worked for a major utility. Rather than use a hotel we booked a cottage through Country Cottages (a holiday cottage leasing company). This meant that everyone had to cook, wash up and generally look after themselves. I did all of the shopping so that this wasn't a distraction. The event lasted three days and was probably the most successful team-building session I've ever done. They really got to know one another. One woman had to go away on the first evening because she didn't want to leave her young son. She stayed the second evening because she felt she had missed so much the previous evening.

'The house idea is a great way of being in control of your own destiny. It has the disadvantage or advantage that if you want anything to happen then you do it yourself. It has the overwhelming advantage of allowing people to be completely themselves.'

Next time you are planning a residential training session with a relatively small group, consider the benefits of using a house.

Getting away from it all

The whole point of having a residential course is to get away from everyday distractions and focus on the content. But how realistic a picture is that in a typical conference hotel? You are constantly aware of the other guests and have to limit your activities or be prepared to irritate them (see page 63). You are restricted by the hotel's meal timings and room allocations. You can't avoid the hubbub of the ordinary world. More subtly, the attendees don't really get away from it all because they have too much privacy. Able to go and hide in their rooms, they can watch TV, telephone back to the office and generally behave as if they aren't on an intensive course at all.

Compare this with a session in a country cottage. There are no other guests, and you can do whatever you like provided it doesn't attract the attention of the police. Meal times and how you use each room (and the garden) is up to you. If you want, you can be totally removed from the world. And it's up to you how much your trainees can escape. There probably won't be TVs in the bedrooms and you can be more prescriptive about how the trainees behave. They'll never feel that they're away from the course just because they're in their bedrooms. Of course some might find this irritating or even claustrophobic, but for an intensive course there is no parallel.

Choose your location

Inevitably hotel locations are relatively limited. Unless you go for a country house hotel, you are likely to be in a town or city. When it comes down to it, one hotel is much like another. Hiring a cottage or house is a different prospect. There is a much wider range to choose from, not just in the variety of locations but even in the nature of the building. You can hire anything from an old lighthouse to a converted barn, from a chocolate-box thatched-roofed idyll to a minimalist dream. There is so much more opportunity with a house or cottage to match the location to the requirements of the course.

Interdependence

One of the ideal applications of a house location is any form of training that involves team building. In a hotel, guests are essentially individual units, cared for by a central staff. In a house, inhabitants are a team, like it or not, as they cope with the everyday tasks from cooking breakfast to locking up at night. This forced interdependence, and the inevitable living at close quarters, can work marvels for team building – or any other training where interdependence is important.

Fun and energy

Like it or not, most conference hotels are dull. They may be comfortable, they may be luxurious and pamper you with exquisite seven-course meals. But all that does for you is put your trainees to sleep. If one of the prime requirements for good training, especially *Training+*, is energy, then a traditional hotel is almost entirely a negative contributor.

Things are very different in the house. The confined spaces actively generate energy. There is much less artificial formality, hence more opportunity for fun. Your evening meal might mean a trip to the local curry house, or a take-away, or a meal where everyone does their bit – whichever is the case, it can be more relaxed yet less lethargy inducing. Initially, for a short period of time, the house may generate nervousness and embarrassment, but this will soon turn over into creative fun.

Control and flexibility

As course organizer, there is only so much control you can exert in a hotel. The hotel staff have their own responsibilities and areas of control. In a house, your control can be near absolute. If you want to turn night into day and sleep until dusk, or turn all the furniture upside down, or hold a seminar in the loo or combine a teaching session with some cookery, you can. The only restraints are physical, legal and getting the house back in the condition you found it in at the end of the session. In practice it is liable to be your imagination that provides the biggest constraint.

Flexibility comes not only from this added level of self-determination, but also from the nature of the accommodation. In a hotel you will typically have a set of identical bedrooms, one or more cloned meeting rooms and possibly access to some of the communal space. In a house each room is liable to be different in terms of furniture, shape and size. The fixtures and fittings of the bathroom and kitchen make them very different. The loft is an adventure waiting to happen. And then there's the garden and any sheds or outhouses or garages that may be out there.

Cost

Money rears its head here as elsewhere. It has to – however much we'd like it to be the case, money just isn't available for training the way it should be. So there's an added bonus that renting a place actually costs less than hotel accommodation.

Against these benefits, as the consultant points out, you have to set doing everything yourself: arranging insurance; catering; providing equipment for sessions, from projectors to pencils; programming all the time, rather than just training sessions. Even so, compared with the benefits these are trivial disadvantages. If you run small residential sessions like this and don't try using a house, you haven't moved on to *Training+*.

Using a hellhole

We would all like to choose the ideal room for training. Unfortunately, the real world is full of make-do training rooms that are far from perfect. It's up to you to make sure that you make the best of what you can get.

Black Hole of Calcutta

While giving training sessions in a large company a few years ago, a training team was frequently allocated a room colloquially known as the Black Hole of Calcutta. This was a rectangular room with a low ceiling that seated around 25 people. In the middle of the building, it had no windows. The air conditioning was less than adequate and the room often overheated.

Faced with the room for the first time, the team did the best they could, propping the door open and encouraging the trainees to move around as much as possible. Even so, the feedback almost universally complained about the room. The next time the team used the room they came prepared. Large, colourful posters were put up on the walls – effectively window substitutes. More cold drinks were provided. To decrease the oppressive feeling, they also scattered sheets of paper around the walls with quotes that looked at the world in different ways. There were significantly fewer complaints next time around.

There are broadly two situations in which you can be landed with a black hole. It may be that you have no warning, or that you have a chance to prepare. Let's take each separately.

Without warning, there is a limit to your ability to mitigate the impact of the environment. You arrive in a new location, perhaps an hour before your trainees, and find that the room is unpleasant. What can you do? A starting point is to have some basic preparation. Carry with you as much as you can to overcome the poor facilities. Here's a typical check list. You might not manage all of this (especially if you are travelling to a remote location by train), but a cut-down pack is always possible:

● No windows – take a couple of colourful posters. Print interesting quotes, relevant texts, etc on fancy paper samples.

- No phone – carry a mobile and make trainees aware that they can use it in an emergency.
- No whiteboard or flip chart – carry a portable flip chart or roll-up whiteboard. Take whiteboard pens and adhesive putty to stick output up on walls.
- No overhead projector or computer projector – take your own. If this is not practical, take a prepared flip chart as fallback.
- No notepaper for attendees – take pads.
- Poor catering – take a carton of milk (to replace nasty powdered milk) and biscuits.

Other actions can be taken with what is on the ground. Be prepared to stick your own notices around the site pointing towards the training room if attendees might have difficulty finding it. Prop the door open if the air conditioning doesn't work and it's not too noisy outside. Generally it isn't practical to do more than patch up the environment before getting started. But don't leave the trainees thinking that you are ignoring their plight. Explain what you have already done and what more might be done. At the first break, contact any local support staff and try to get changes made. If there is any danger of your using the location again, write to those responsible for the room and highlight the problems.

Where you have advance warning of a site that has problems, more can be done. Consider hiring in extra equipment (from projectors to portable air conditioning). Bring appropriate specific requirements with you. It's tempting to leave things as they are and blame the accommodation provider rather than trying to sort it out. After all, your responsibility is the training, not the accommodation. The trouble is, the effectiveness of your training will drop off if the environment is poor. You owe it to yourself and your trainees to fight for the best practical environment.

4B **COMMUNICATION**

A core element of much training is the presentation. This can be anything from a talking head to a full-scale, multimedia assault on the senses. Yet we've all got bored of the same old bullet point slides (in yellow or white on dark blue, perhaps allowing a little red for emphasis). A presentation is fundamentally theatre – and trainers need to take an appropriate stance to make sure that it's good theatre. Beyond the formal presentation, all training involves communication. It's at the core of our business and cannot be ignored.

For practical reasons we tend to 'chunk up' training into sizeable portions. There are increasing opportunities, though, for bite-sized training, from 'Instant' books to lunchtime sessions and just-in-time training or training on demand. As more people move to manage their own time effectively across a portfolio of responsibilities, the ability to use incremental training will become more and more valuable. Methods of chunking material appear among the communication sections.

A final, often ignored aspect that comes into communication is the fact that both trainer and trainees are human beings. It sounds such an unremarkable observation, yet the impact on how we communicate is significant. Taking this into account in the approach taken to training can make a lot of difference.

Key topic – Energy transfer

Of all the generics that can be communicated to your trainees – facts, feelings, concepts, structures, skills and more – the one most likely to be overlooked, but almost impossible to do without, is energy. Energy is the oil of training, a meta-requirement without which any other objectives are likely to fail.

Energy injection

Nic Cope is an IT manager who also is a highly successful choir conductor and musical director. He finds that Friday evening choir practices often require an energy injection on a level that exceeds many other training environments. The attendees have just finished a long, hard week at work, and would probably rather be in the pub than where they are. They certainly don't want to be bothered to put the effort into singing that is necessary to make the difference between an average performance and an excellent one.

Nic uses a range of exercises and techniques to get energy into a choir. He has them performing physical exercises. He will distribute individuals around the building, singing towards the wall. He will introduce challenges and humour. He is constantly on the move himself, bouncing around and putting physical energy into his conducting. Some of the attendees find this diffi-cult. One middle-aged woman was heard to observe that she didn't like his style, because she'd had enough after a hard week and couldn't cope with his leaping about the place. Nic, according to her, had altogether too much energy. But in fact she was proving the point. What she felt uncomfortable with was the injection of energy that dragged her out of comfortable lethargy. Like it or not, the choir was being given an energy boost.

If there's one thing that the rest of the world can learn from the greats in the training arena, it's energy transfer. Communication isn't always about facts and figures, or even feelings. A key aspect of the communication between trainer and trainees is being able to bring the trainees to life, forcing energy into them. Some of this will come from exercises. As we see in *Warm-ups* (page 130), it is possible to give a group an exercise to do that is both enjoyable and capable of increasing personal energy.

Sometimes the solution is even simpler. A sugar boost (sweets or biscuits, for example) will give an immediate but short-lived jolt of energy. When you are aiming to overcome lethargy induced by bad air conditioning or simply sitting still for too long, getting the trainees up and moving, preferably in cool fresh air, can be enough to increase energy levels. This doesn't have to involve frenetic activity – just making sure that, for instance, getting refreshments involves getting up from the seat and walking around the room can help.

However, for much of a training session, the level of energy in your trainees will depend on your personal energy level and how you communicate it. There's a bit of a domino effect here. You will need to make sure that your energy levels are good to be able to communicate energy to your trainees during the day. After a good training session you should feel physically drained, but emotionally uplifted. This means that you owe it to yourself to be in good shape before giving a training session. It's not over the top to look at yourself as an athlete, needing to prepare for a competition. You owe it to yourself to have a good night's sleep and a sensible diet.

Assuming you are full of energy yourself, you then need to look at ways to communicate that energy without using too much of it up. If you needed to lose a unit of energy for each unit you give to each individual you would soon be drained. But there is plenty that can be done to leverage the energy transfer. Use your eyes, your tone, your posture to convey energy, rather than jumping around all the time (though there's nothing wrong with some energetic movement). Watch a good TV actor – see how much can be conveyed with changes of expression. Widening your eyes, putting enthusiasm and variety of expression into your tone, not slumping but using your body to convey what you are saying, will all give energy.

You should also look at *what* you are saying. While a good actor can put across a shopping list with oodles of energy, most of us will be helped by the right words. Positive expressions, plenty of adjectives and adverbs, and regular stories from life can all help to increase the energy content of your material. Jargon and long entangled sentences have the opposite effect of reducing energy. And look at how your sentences are formed. Short, punchy sentences, sometimes a single sentence to empha-size a point, good dramatic pauses (but not too long) – all these can enhance the energy in your communication.

Finally, look at where your words come from. You only have to watch a TV newsreader switch from the autocue to reading from paper to see a drop in the amount of energy that is communicated. Speaking without reading the text has the maximum energy, autocue next, and a speech written on paper last of all. I'm not actually advocating working without notes – but unless you have to use an autocue they should be keyword notes that can bring you back on track and make sure everything is covered, not word-for-word text to read.

Any training session has an energy curve, sometimes peaking, some-times drifting along the bottom. You can't keep a group of people at maximum energy for too long – inevitably they will burn out. Achieving the ideal on the energy front is not about pure injection but about managing energy. Although it's more common to need to push energy up, you will occasionally have to pull it down. Perhaps a group is in an interactive session and is firing on all cylinders, pumping out ideas. You need to do something with those ideas and to move on. Sometimes a little dampener will be beneficial.

Even conventional times for energizers aren't necessarily right. As Margaret Parkin points out in the excellent *Tales for Trainers* (see Appendix, page 184), most trainers pull out a warm-up exercise after lunch to jolt the trainees back into activity. But there's a good reason why we're low on energy in the 'graveyard shift' – our body has shifted blood to the stomach to aid digestion. Is the answer really to get people bouncing up and down? Not unless your aim is to sell indigestion tablets. A more natural activity would be to lie down and have a nap. This might not fit with your schedule, but Parkin suggests that this is a good time to use a story, to make use of the halfway-to-sleep brainwave patterns to powerfully instil a message in the minds of the trainees.

We have successfully used more sedentary timeouts after lunch, rather than high-energy warm-ups. But the discovery that it isn't always appro-priate to get the trainees bouncing around the place doesn't invalidate the message. Communicating energy is as essential as information. The right energy injections at the right time can make all the difference between success and failure.

Slides that scintillate

Visual aids are important. While there are times when simply talking without any visual aids can put across a message more clearly, there are good reasons why in most circumstances visual aids will make a presentation or training session better. It's a shame, then, that so many visual aids are poor.

You can't see this, but...

In the past year I have attended a good number of presentations, all by professionals, many trying to train or educate. In a horribly large percentage of cases, the presentation goes something like this:

Puts up first slide. 'I'm Sarah Jones from InTrain, and I'm going to take you through the basics of handling VAT. I just need to...' she moves on three slides, overshoots, presses what she thinks is the 'back up' key only to be dropped into the PowerPoint editing screen and finally gets to the slide she wants. 'This is where I fit in the company and how we are organized.' There follows a series of slides with information that no one present except Ms Jones has any interest in whatsoever. 'Right. This shows the VAT return form. I'm sorry it's so small. You can't actually read it, but what it says here is...' We'll draw a veil over the proceedings. Slide after slide 'it's difficult to make this out' or 'you can't see this, but...' Scintillating it is not.

Making visual aids so much better is not rocket science. In fact it shouldn't be necessary to put it in *Training+*, it should be everyday knowledge. Yet the number of times I'm faced with 'you can't see this, but...' tells me something different. And there are opportunities to go beyond the typical presentation, however professional it may be. If you consider the level of visual input that most audiences are familiar with, most presentations have just about reached the era of lantern slides. We see a series of images, which may have a small amount of animation to make the point. All too often, the slides are even worse than images – a mass of words. But I'm not going to hammer the 'few words on a slide, use images' line, we've all heard that and ignored it too often.

The time has come to move on the model on which the presentation is based. We should not be looking to lantern slides, but to TV, magazines and Web sites as the basis for our presentations. Always be on the lookout to learn from these ferociously competitive media. They are all in the business of communicating key information quickly. That's what your support media is for, too. So why do most of us ignore the lessons that TV, magazines and latterly the Web have painfully learnt?

Fashion gurus

Whatever the medium, you will find that visual styles change. Old styles cease to be fashionable; new styles come in. Surely we should be above the vagaries of fashion? Think again. Whenever a TV programme or magazine or Web site changes design there will initially be moans. 'It's not how I'm used to it, so I don't like it.' But leave it too long and it will look tired, out of date and boring. In the four years I have been writing for one of the big computing magazines, it has gone through two major redesigns. Looking back at the older issues, the style looks archaic now. The same is true when you see archive footage of TV shows that are still in production.

My company's practice with presentations is to change the design about once a year. This keeps the look fresh, and with modern presentation graphics programs there is no problem in changing the underlying look of all the slides in a presentation at a stroke. For the look of our slides we consider advertising, TV graphics and more. Last year's slides had a stark black background with white lettering all in lower case. Punctuation was picked out in red. This year we're using a grey image of a leaf on a crinkly bark background. This has a darker grey semi-transparent overlay on which the yellow text appears. Next year... who knows?

Along with the general look goes the font to be used. In general, san-serif fonts like Helvetica work better on screen, while serif fonts like Times Roman work better on paper. Presentation fonts should not be too jazzy or difficult to read, but be prepared to try out a good range of fonts against your backdrop before you are happy you've reached the right one. It's best to stick to one or two fonts in a presentation unless you are aiming for the naïve designer look of splattering a whole range of different fonts (some not quite straight) on the page – but this has to be used with great care, as the borderline between designer mess and the real thing is very narrow.

Before deciding on your new presentation look, get a pile of magazines from the glossy end of the market – fashion and lifestyle. Look how the text is laid out on the first page of features and in the bigger ads. Look too at the advertising and other text on TV. And cruise round a few of the hottest professional Web sites, being prepared to steal any look that works and says 'this year' for you. Sad to say as a book writer, one place it's probably best not to look is the covers of books, which have too long a lead time to be particularly up to date – even so, most book covers are streets ahead of presentations, so you might still get some inspiration.

Colour coordinates

In developing your presentations, use of colour is important. Again fashion will typically dictate a palette that really works at the moment. Look for the colours that are popular in clothing and in graphics. As I write, grey is very popular in fashion, while desert colours (sand, setting sun red, etc) are hot in TV graphics. I'm not suggesting there is any need to be a fanatical follower of fashion, but for those of us who aren't designers it's a quick and easy way of getting a colour scheme that is liable to go down well.

You do, of course, have to consider the basics of colour coordination for legibility. Magazines can get away with much worse colour mixes than a screen before the text becomes unreadable. You have to be more careful. Some general guidance:

● Don't use too many colours (except in colour pictures, and even then it can be effective to reduce them to, say, shades of blue). Only use very bright colours to emphasize a point.
● Use blue, black or grey as background. This is the ideal in terms of legibility on a screen, but it doesn't have to be set in concrete. If, for instance, you fancied using this year's hot TV graphics colours you might have a sand-coloured background with a semi-transparent rectangle darkening it where the text is, or a blood red, setting sun colour.

- Avoid yellow and red in the periphery, as colour sight has trouble with this. This is only really a problem if your presentation is to be viewed on individual screens in front of the trainee — most distant large screens don't operate in the periphery of vision.
- Don't rely on colour alone to differentiate detail — use shape too. Otherwise mixing effects can result in confusion.
- Similarly, don't rely on colour to define edges; use lines.
- Use redundant coding (don't depend on colour alone to indicate something). It's fine to have a list where green items are 'go' and red items are 'stop', but you need to be aware that there are enough colour-blind people (men especially) in the population that you will have some in any sizeable audience. Use a graphic or layout as well as the colour.
- Similar colours should denote similar meaning. If you are going to use colour to indicate something, use it consistently throughout the presentation.
- Use high-contrast colour combinations for text. Legibility depends on the contrast between the letters and the background, not on absolute brightness. Avoid colour combinations that jar, such as red lettering on a blue background.

Moving pictures

There is no doubt that moving pictures put across a stronger image than a static image. You only have to look at the impact of TV. But that impact is a two-edged sword, because we have become accustomed to the quality of professional broadcasting. If you look at a videotape from TV in the 1950s you will see just how much things have moved on. To think that you can make a home movie-style video and take on the professionals is to live in cloud cuckoo land. Yet video is a powerful medium, so how can you sensibly incorporate it?

The easiest approach is to buy it in. Use a professional piece of video to illustrate your point. There's nothing new about this, but a good snippet of video (provided it's not more than 15 minutes long) can still give a real boost to a presentation. If you want to do it yourself, stick to the formats of professional broadcasting where an amateurish presentation is still acceptable. Look at programmes using home video clips for entertainment or to illustrate natural disasters. Or keep things intensely simple – a series of quickie head and shoulder shots talking to camera with no attempt to link them with narration can work very well. See *Hollywood or bust*, page 60, for more on the use of video.

Instant images

Since the end of the 1990s the trainer has had a new resource – the digital camera. With prices that are affordable in most training budgets, these compact cameras record directly into a digital format acceptable by a PC. We have found these a very effective aid in livening up presentations in sessions that last a day or longer. Take pictures of your trainees as they arrive and when they are engaged in exercises – the more entertaining they look during the exercises the better.

You can slot the images into a pre-prepared presentation. This can then run as part of the programme later in the session. For instance it might be shown after lunch when the trainees return to the training room, or first thing on the morning of the second day, or to close at the end of the session. This simple act brings the trainees into the presentation, making it more 'their' session and achieving an astonishing level of buy-in for the investment of a little time to fit the photos in place.

Follow the news

For a single source that gives some of the best guidance on presentations watch prime-time TV news. The newscaster's role is not dissimilar to your own. He or she has to put across a complex topic in a memorable way in the minimum of time. You will probably have the luxury of more time, but it's instructive to see just how much can be achieved, while keeping your attention, in a short time.

The TV newscaster is, in effect, a talking head like yourself. Newscasters have the advantage of on-the-scene reports, but there is still plenty done using a combination of the newscaster and graphics, whether alongside the person or temporarily replacing him or her on screen. Look how the TV news handles these graphics in terms of visual content and style, and how they put across text when they have to. Take in the news from several channels to get a good cross-section of styles. If possible, try out a different culture's news too – US-based readers should try to get access to the BBC or similar stations; Europeans should try CNN.

Speaking to the masses

For all the sophistication of modern technology, training often comes down to one person talking to a group of others – sometimes a very big group. The modern focus on the team and the benefits of small groups makes cosy interactive sessions very attractive, but there is still a place for pure public speaking in training.

> **He is one of those orators of whom it was well said, 'Before they get up, they do not know what they are going to say; when they are speaking, they do not know what they are saying; and when they have sat down, they do not know what they have said.'**
>
> *Sir Winston Churchill of Lord Charles Beresford*

There's often an assumption that a pure talking head is to be avoided at all costs. The drivers of this assumption are complex. TV has shown us that talking heads are boring – we need fast-changing moving pictures. Without effective presentation graphics there is no way we can get a message across. And, frankly, modern audiences simply can't take someone just standing there and talking to them. It's sad, but that's the way it is – they're butterflies with no attention span.

Maybe. Or maybe those who are determined to shoot down the unsupported speaker are misjudging their audiences, based on dubious information. Go along to see a good story-telling comedian. Not someone who delivers a string of one-liners, but a performer whose humour depends on natural observation, spiced with a touch of absurdity. Sit down and listen, and have an evening disappear. The comedian could be on stage for two hours, and you've had a great time. And what has the comedian done? Just talked to you. Practically no visual aids, and if there are any, simple props to make a point. Nothing high tech. Yet your attention was held. How did the comedian manage it? If you have ever seen such a comedian perform, or seen a show like this on TV, spend a minute thinking about what it was that kept your interest.

First and foremost, humour. Isolated humour is very difficult to do. Most actors find slapstick or telling a joke hard work – non-professionals find it even harder. Don't try it. But you can still make use of story-telling humour. Without stealing the thunder of using storytelling as a training vehicle (see *I want to tell you a story* on page 97), your best bet in bringing humour into a training session is in the context of a real-life (or near-real – be prepared to embroider) story. It can be a war story, showing the need for the training or showing examples of getting it right (or wrong). It can be a story directly related to the material – but make sure that your trainees are regularly entertained.

That isn't all, though. The comedian makes use of timing and tone to vary the delivery. Sometimes loud, sometimes hectoring, sometimes quiet and reasonable. The tone of delivery is essentially theatrical, something you can't afford to miss out on if you are going to deliver training as a speaker. And comedians split up their material. There are some longer stories, but many are quite short. Don't overload the brain with too complex a story – keep the punch lines coming.

The final great comedians' technique is content. What they say is interesting – you want to know what happens next – and entertaining. Quite unreasonably these are criteria that seem rarely applied to training materials, which it is often assumed should be dry as dust. To some extent I blame the tradition that academic papers should be objective, impersonal and boring. This spread into business report writing and from there into training. It doesn't have to be this way.

Of course, the comedian isn't the only model you can use. There is the good after-dinner speaker who can deliver excellent, serious content but keeps up a constant flow of stories to support it, or the good vicar's sermon that intrigues, fascinates and challenges, rather than puts the congregation to sleep. The role models are there – and so is the opportunity. Try to get the chance to do an after-dinner speech or a comedy spot in a talent show. Learn from the experience where you need to improve your skills for training purposes. And always be on the lookout for bringing in a story and some humour. It stops the trainees getting bored and helps fix the thoughts in memory, which can't be bad.

The opportunities for pure speaking are still valuable. It's not a replacement for all the fancy stuff. I am not saying you should throw away your video projector. But sometimes, especially when the message is story-based, a speaker can put across a message with human depth that no slide or high-tech support can rival. It takes practice, it takes skill, but good public speaking should be in the *Training+* armoury.

Hollywood or bust

Video is now a readily available commodity. Making a video to support a training session is much less expensive than it once was. Consider the benefits of DIY.

Vox Pop

Faced with training a group of customer service staff, a small training company took a modern video camera out amongst the customers and pulled in a wide range of comments about the service given by the client company. They also asked the senior management of the company what they thought about the customer service staff, their conditions and their customers.

The best of these video clips, ruthlessly edited down to a few seconds each, were accumulated into three very short videos (around two minutes per video). These were shown first thing, after lunch and near the end. The cost was tiny compared with the impact these shots made.

Using bespoke video in training need not be expensive. There is no doubt that moving pictures have a visual impact that no end of slides can't deliver. But there needs to be an awareness that the use of video puts you into direct comparison with the professionals. TV's everyday slickness has brought us a level of expectation that is much higher than can generally be achieved by an amateur. However, there are some classes of video that can stand alone without such concerns.

To achieve such a video needs relatively low-cost equipment. A sensible minimum would be a video camera, tripod, separate microphone and basic lighting. Post-processing needs to be done – you can't sensibly edit your video in the camera. You might be able to manage this cleanly enough with good modern equipment simply by copying to a VHS player, but if this doesn't work well enough, consider getting a short session with professional help in a video-editing suite.

The most common, but still very effective use in training is the Vox Pop – getting the input of an individual or individuals who can't actually be there on the day but can make an effective input to the training. This might be framing comments, as in the mini-case above. Alternatively, it could be a case of bringing in an expert or celebrity who can't be there on the day. For example, before domestic video existed, I was giving some training on the basics of artificial intelligence to a group of programmers. I arranged to see one of the top professors on the subject and filmed a short interview with him on 8 millimetre movie film. This interview was used to open the session, input by a recognized expert that was greatly appreciated by the trainees.

Alternatively, the video can be used to show context images. For instance, where the training is specific to the workplace, but the session is held elsewhere, it can be useful to show a video of the application on site. Another very effective use is in showing disasters associated with the topic of the training. At IBM's usability centre in the UK they have been known to show a video taken during the usability testing of a bank's computer system.

The innocent bank manager in the video is supposed to follow instructions on a card to use his new banking PC. First he is told to log-in – but without being shown how to switch the machine on. After pushing various buttons he finds the big red switch on the front of the system unit and powers up the PC – but not the screen. It is an old IBM design that had the monitor power switch out of sight behind the casing. As he tries to turn it on, the manager presses various keys on his keyboard. Finally he finds the screen switch. At last he can type in his password as it says on the card – only he has unwittingly already typed a set of characters. One step ahead, he doesn't manage to log on, and after 45 minutes gives up in disgust.

IBM's video is an object lesson for hardware designers, the writers of instruction books and the writers of computer software. It is also very entertaining. Such videos of customers trying to deal with your company, of staff trying to cope with your management edicts and so forth can be highly effective motivators in a training environment – and usually provide light relief too. We learn a lesson, but laugh at the same time.

Videos can also be used as a feedback mechanism to show trainees how they perform. This has been done often enough that most trainees are aware of the possibility – and most of them hate it. This is so much the case that it is usually necessary to put a group of trainees at ease if they come into a training room and see a video camera in the corner, assuring them that they are not going to be videoed. There are no special consid-erations here, except to note that to be really effective you need to be prepared to spend the evening in a frantic editing session and only play strictly edited highlights to make the points you require – otherwise the training fly-on-the-wall video combines embarrassment and boredom in equal parts.

A final use of video that can be considered is as a vehicle for trainees to feed back to other trainees. Splitting trainees into small groups who learn something and then feed back to the others is very effective, but can be hackneyed. Giving the trainees the opportunity to feed back through video is one way to give them more flexibility and interest value, provided you give them some tight guidelines. There should be limits on timing (both playback and the time to make the video – video filming can eat up time). They should keep things simple. And they should avoid trying to be funny. Their amateurism will ensure that a serious presentation comes across with some humour – any attempt to make it funny, unless superbly done, will simply come across as childish.

Giving it all you've got

Half-hearted training produces half-hearted results. You have to be prepared to go the extra mile to make your training effective. Sometimes this means treading on other people's toes. It is often worth it.

Quiet team-building

It was just before Christmas. A consultant was briefed to give a team of about 40 people a team-building session that was a raucous kick-off to the Christmas party. The consultant called the hotel and explained what he would be doing. He explained that he would be making a lot of noise and this could be disruptive. They said that there was no problem with this.

The consultant turned up early as usual and found that the room was one of these with a fibreboard partition splitting a larger room into two. He spoke to the woman who was setting up next door – she had a conference on pharmaceutical distribution. This did not sound promising. The consultant explained what he was going to be doing and she said that the partition was fine.

They started slowly. After about an hour the session had built up to the point where they were playing silly games and were frankly being outrageous. The woman organizing the next-door conference stormed into the session, came up to the consultant at the front, and started laying into him. The consultant had just finished explaining the next task, so he told everyone to carry on without him and led the conference organizer forcibly out of the room. She said that her conference was having difficulty because of the noise. The consultant said that he knew they would, and had warned both the hotel and her. She said that the team-building session had to stop. The consultant said no. He told her to take it up with the hotel.

By lunchtime the conference next door had closed down, had been completely packed up and had left. There was a note on the door saying 'Conference cancelled due to noisy neighbours'.

In the case study, the consultant was not prepared to go for the half-hearted approach his neighbour was demanding. He went for it, giving it all he had. The result might have irritated the neighbour, but the attendees were delighted, and the session was very successful. All too often, a training session has that wet-lettuce feel of lack of commitment. It's time for an action plan of total immersion.

The Mousetrap effect

Sometimes the trainer seems to be suffering from the *Mousetrap* effect. You know the sort of thing. Imagine being in the same play for three years. You are about to go on stage for your 1179th performance. You don't have to think about it – you could do it in your sleep, and on the whole you do. Not surprisingly, the audience is not fooled. You put across all the enthusiasm of a sleepwalker.

It can be the same with training. It's all very well if you have a wide portfolio and are doing different courses every week, but how about the poor trainer who has a whole season of the same old course? Day after day, the same message, yet somehow it has to be fresh and vibrant and I'm asking you to give your all. Don't despair. It is possible. It's not always easy, but it is possible.

Returning for a moment to the theatrical model, some plays manage to keep running for years and still give the audience a jolt. I don't know how long Sir Andrew Lloyd Webber's *Cats* has been going in London's West End, but the cast continues to give the audience the feel of something special. They aren't just going through the motions. What's the difference? In part it's turnover. The cast of *Cats* changes quite regularly. If you have to give a course over a long period, find some way of course sharing with other trainers, doing each others' courses to increase interest. But more than this, there is the difference between a performance like *Cats* and a static stage play. The sheer energy of the play makes it very difficult to give a dull performance. If your training is done slumped in a chair in a stuffy room, maybe you will get dull. Get up, move around. You don't have to dance and sing, but make use of physical energy in the way the *Cats* performers do.

As a trainer you've also got some real advantages over the theatrical performer. You can inject much more variety than they can. You can change the way you present the course, change the materials, change order – keep things fresh by rotation, like crop rotation in the fields. You are in much more control than in a scripted performance. And you also have the advantage of much more direct audience participation. Okay, to some extent all the trainees for a particular course may tend to be the same kind of people, but get down to the real person and there is plenty of individuality. Revel in the unique character of the people you are privileged to meet every day. Sounds forced? Maybe it is to start with, but try it and you will find it is true. People are interesting, and despite broad patterns, people are different. Don't see it as a hundred identical sessions, but a hundred opportunities to meet a new and different group of people.

Morning after

It was a great night, but you were up until three in the morning, then had to get up at seven to catch the train (which of course was late) and frankly, you are knackered. Outcome? Training that lacks a certain something. When the trainees are feeding back, that something might even be consciousness. It's very hard to make do with insufficient sleep, to be worn out, and still to give a great course.

There's a time management issue here. You've got to decide what is important. If you want to be a great trainer, if you want your courses to be *Training+*, not just the everyday variety, you have got to be prepared to give something in return. I'm not asking for hours of preparation – just that you get enough sleep. After a few days of getting what your body needs (not an arbitrary eight hours, or what you can fit in), you will be surprised how much easier it is to give it your all. Trivial? Maybe, but few people realize just how much their performance tails off when they have insufficient sleep – and that is the condition most of us are in. Of course there is a host of reasons. It's not just partying all night. It might be the children. It might be noise from next door. I can't sort all this for you, merely point out the consequences.

Don't blame me, I'm just the trainer

A good catch-all excuse when a session doesn't go very well is that the trainees simply weren't up to it. You were happy to do anything and everything, but it was like trying to stir porridge with a piece of paper.

There's an element of truth in this. Sometimes a group of trainees aren't exactly motivated. But that's no excuse for not giving your all – and as we have seen on page 50, you can inject a lot of your energy into the attendees. It may take a little time, but the trainees will start to put their all into it if you do. It's infectious.

What do you expect from an arts graduate?

Or whatever. If you are a professional trainer you will sometimes find yourself training in a subject that you know little about. It's inevitable. You end up with that well-known syndrome where you are one chapter ahead in the textbook of everyone else, relying on the same knowledge sources as they have for your information. When you are struggling to keep up, how can you realistically give your all?

In practice, this is a less powerful argument than it may seem. Provided you can bring a childlike interest to bear on the subject, you can easily break through. Talk to children about a topic they have encountered for the first time at school (at least, children who are still young enough not to have been brainwashed into thinking that it's not cool to be interested in anything). They are full of it, glowing with the interest and novelty of what they have learned. The topic can be quite mundane; the fact is, they know something new and want to impart it. So what's your problem? The topic is new to you, but with the right attitude any subject can be interesting. Anything can capture your imagination, if you let it. Break away from the textbook. Use the World Wide Web and other sources to read up on the subject. Talk to people. You might be an arts graduate, but you can still find what Tom Peters refers to as WOW! in the workings of an engineering tool or the statistics of market segmentation. Just see it the right way.

No time, no time!

We've already encountered a time management problem in getting enough sleep. It's a part of the wider problem – having enough time. It's all very well to expect you to give a session with your whole heart and mind, but in practice you are trying to work out what to say in tomorrow morning's seminar in your spare time, and when you aren't thinking about that you've got a meeting to organize. And the dog to collect from the vet's. And aren't you cooking tonight?

A quick visit to the time management first aid kit is called for. This doesn't mean going on courses and buying the book and the T-shirt – it's about getting a clear set of personal objectives and a handful of priorities for the week, then making them very visible and always bearing them in mind. With that in operation, it's time to learn from Casanova.

It is said (personally I wouldn't know) that the great lovers have one thing in common: the ability to concentrate wholeheartedly on their current conquest, to focus tightly on that one person, to really give them everything. Of course 10 minutes later it might be someone entirely different, but for that moment there's no faking; the object of affection is the centre of the universe. To carry your time management into the training arena, you need to practise that singular focus. Don't let anything else enter your thoughts. If you have to have a different focus brought to your attention (for example the need to go to lunch), give the responsibility to someone else (or a mechanical aid like an alarm). Time might be a problem, but it is going to march on at the same speed what-ever you do. What you can do is manage your focus – and make the session you are involved in the only thing you are thinking about at the time.

Do it for yourself

Much of the above has been about how you can make your training better by giving it your all. Realistically, if you are going to give so much, we have to ask what's in it for you? Surprisingly, quite a lot. There is plenty of evidence that people who have a real input into the content of their jobs are less stressed than the rest. If you have a session that really takes off, you will get a real kick out of it too – the benefits aren't just for the trainees. And it isn't exactly going to harm your career prospects if people are coming out of your sessions enthusing about them. In the end, though, this is going to be something you are doing for a chunk of time – that's time you won't get back for good behaviour. If you give it your all, you will enjoy it more. Surely there's no more to be said?

Non-verbals

There is rarely enough consideration given to non-verbal communication in the training environment, yet as a communication issue it is second to none.

Silent session

In a training session for would-be creativity trainers and facilitators, we often have a short period where a pair of trainee facilitators have to manage a discussion without speaking at all. The rest of the course know what's going on, and have been known either to play up or to be excessively polite as a result of it, but the exercise has some interesting outcomes.

We all know in theory how significant the non-verbal side is to communication, but it's only when you see it in action that you can get a real feel for it. The participants often feel that their non-verbal techniques are clumsy, emphasizing how much they need more practice at using them. They also invariably forget audible non-verbal communication, resorting to mime. Of course, the whole situation is entirely artificial, and some of the discomfort comes from this, but it's also surprising just how restricted many younger people, particularly in the UK, are about using their non-verbal communication to the full. It's hard to imagine having the same problems (say) in Italy.

Giving your non-verbal skills a check-up is advisable for anyone in the training business. Unless you are particularly good at taking a step back and watching yourself from the outside, it's probably best to put together a check-list of skills and look out for each in turn rather than analysing the whole spectrum simultaneously. The process can, of course, be helped if you can video yourself in action, then review the video at a later date. For each of the suggested key headings below, check out what you are doing and have a go at tuning up your performance. These headings aren't exclusive – feel free to add your own as well.

Posture

What does your typical training posture say about you? Do you have an open posture, standing well balanced, arms away from the front of your body? Or is your posture closed, arms crossed, sitting down, head bowed? Achieving openness is essential to getting the message across effectively; otherwise, like it or not, your trainees won't trust you. Do you stand rooted to the spot when you speak? Do you jiggle about from foot to foot? (This is something I find hard not to do.) Aim for a comfortable stance with regular shifts, but without constant bobbing about.

Using a projector, whiteboard or flip chart

When involved in training using a projector, whiteboard or flip chart, how do you position yourself? Do you lose eye contact with the trainees? How do you point to the screen or chart? Is there a way to do this without turning your back on the audience? When you are noting down comments from the trainees, do you write and then turn back to them with an open body position, encouraging further input?

Using hands

How do you use your hands during a session? How comfortable do you feel about the way you use your hands? Ensure that you put down any pen or pointer, so you are not constantly fiddling with it. Do you use open hands to help bring people into a conversation? Do you use hand movements to emphasize your words when speaking? If these are not natural to you (that is, you are doing them because you are aware of the impact of body language), are you using broad, stage gestures or tiny nervous gestures? Do you keep your hands away from your face? Do you make sure your hands are relaxed, not making fists?

Using eyes

When presenting, do you sweep the audience with your eyes, bringing as many as possible in? Do you use your eyes to encourage someone to make (or continue making, or stop making) a contribution – by looking directly at them, raising the eyebrows, widening the eyes? Do you maintain eye contact with someone who is speaking if you want to keep them speaking and break eye contact if you'd like them to shut up?

Using position in the room

Do you stay stuck on your podium, or do you actively use the space in the room? Do you move towards someone to get them to speak more quietly and personally, or move away to get them to speak louder? Do you move amongst the audience to keep them on their toes?

Touching

This is a difficult one. Not only does touching come naturally to some people while being incredibly difficult for others, but there are severe restrictions on the amount of touching that is now acceptable in a business format. However, given this proviso, do you use a light touch to encourage someone to contribute or to get them moving?

Using volume and tone

Remember both the volume and tone of your voice as components of your non-verbal communication. Speaking more quietly can help settle down an audience. A sudden shouted statement can give great emphasis if used effectively and sparingly (though such a dramatic approach needs plenty of practice). Use your tone to keep the topic interesting, passing on your own sense of enthusiasm.

Grunts, nods and gestures

Don't forget the whole repertoire of grunts, nods and gestures that form part of your conversational non-verbal communication. Often in the artificial training position these are reduced or removed entirely, but you still need occasionally to encourage others to keep speaking with a 'mm-hh', to nod encouragement and use the whole array of hand signals and gestures to help reinforce your message.

Bite-sized chunks

Too often, training ignores the realities of learning and retention. We know that information is retained better if it is put across in bite-sized chunks and reinforced at gradually lengthening periods – yet a training course all too often consists of sessions that are too long or inappropriately structured.

**Whence is thy learning? Hath thy toil
O'er books consumed the midnight oil?**

John Gay, Fables

Perhaps it's because of the way managers work, but in my experience management training is particularly bad at the twin towers of retention – 'chunking' and reviews. Once you get stuck into a meaty management training issue, it's not unusual to continue for a whole afternoon, or even drift into the evening. But this is ignoring the basic facts we know about the way the brain operates.

Ensure that your training is broken into chunks of no more than an hour – 45 minutes might be better – with short breaks between the chunks. This should be the case even when there's a continuous topic under way. This recovery time should be given over to something completely different, rather than allowing the trainees to stick with the topic. Give them something to do (whether it's getting a coffee or surfing the Net) – don't let them continue the session across the break.

To make sure that this happens, be prepared to actually throw the trainees out of the training room. Tell them you don't want to see them for another four minutes. Be firm – but also explain why you are doing this. It can be quite frustrating when you are firing on all cylinders to have an enforced break, but all the evidence is that it is beneficial.

Look also for opportunities to build reviews into your training process. We're all familiar with the line 'tell them what you're going to tell them, then tell them, then tell them what you just told them' – but here we are looking for longer-term reinforcement. It's generally reckoned that a short review after a few minutes, a day, a week, a month and six months is sensible to lock learning into long-term memory. Such reviews need not be more than a minute or two for a whole session of learning. Look for ways to build reviews into your training process. Have you got mechanisms for sending attendees reminders (say by e-mail) after one day, one week and so forth? Give your trainees calendars with the review dates marked in. Use electronic calendaring to get reminders in their diaries. The possibilities for extended review are there – but it takes organization to use them.

Props

The dividing line between teaching and theatre is narrower than many trainers admit. Information transfer is enhanced by proper use of all the tricks of the theatrical trade, and never more so than with props.

Happy circumstance

A team of development trainers was en route to the location of a team-building exercise that used a war-game format. As they drove up the motorway, they spotted a compound by the road that housed all kinds of military vehicles from armoured cars to full-scale tanks. The opportunity seemed too good to miss. The impact of having an armoured car outside the training venue would be worth any reasonable expenditure. The team pulled off the motorway and headed for the compound.

We look elsewhere (page 33) at making use of what you can find, but this is never more true than with props. Whatever your training session, keep an eye out when you are getting ready at home, when you are en route, when you are in the office preparing, when you are at the training venue – look out for any props that will make the training more effective. In the example above it didn't work out. The caretaker of the compound did not trust the development team; his conversation seemed limited to 'I've got dogs', delivered in an aggressive tone. Still, the idea was great; the opportunity was too good to miss.

More usually, though, your props will be a thought-out part of the exercise. Once you have the basic outline of the training prepared, look through it for opportunities to bring props in. They can be used in a number of ways during a training session.

Context setters

Some props, like the abortive attempt to get hold of a tank in the case study, are purely there to set the scene. These are particularly important in a themed event (see page 30), where appropriate props can make all the difference to encouraging the trainees to get into the spirit of the event. Context setters are not actively used in the training process; it is their presence that makes a contribution rather than any practical use. For this reason, context-setting props need to be appropriately displayed – there's not a lot of point if you can't see them.

Visual aids

A large class of props act as visual aids, illustrating a point or helping make it more memorable. Bearing in mind that the memory fixes best on visual images (the more colourful and outrageous the better), a good prop can really help anchor a concept. It can be as simple as a picture or diagram. It can be a visual extension of the concept. For instance, when teaching de Bono's Six Thinking Hats concept, we use a collection of strange hats rescued from jumble sales, which someone is volunteered to wear while the particular hat is being discussed. The sillier the hat, the more effective the memory aid.

An alternative way to emphasize the point is to have a prop that changes in some way as you use it. When teaching a basic introduction to personal computers, I used to rip apart a diskette to produce the innards and hand them round. I could have had an opened-up diskette ready to show, but the act of ripping it apart added to the impact.

Attention grabbers

There is a special class of visual aid where the whole point of the prop is to regain the audience's attention. It may be that energy levels are dropping. It may be that you have just been through a section of the session that has multiple foci, and there's a need to pull the trainees back to a single point. Such a prop might not have any physical function other than being seen, but is a shock tactic. By producing it suddenly, unexpectedly, the trainees' attention is dragged back to the trainer; their full concentration is suddenly returned. Because of this shock principle, something that actually is shocking (involving a loud noise, a flash, a dismembered body part or the equivalent) is most likely to deliver the result.

Timeouts

Sometimes props can be used in a deliberate process of moving the trainees away from the subject for a short time. This can be very helpful when trying to enforce a break to chunk up the training, or when getting a group to think in a different and more creative way. At such a time, physical puzzles and exercises involving physical objects can be particularly effective. Not only do you get the mind working in a different way, but the physical movement required helps get energy back into a flagging group. For more on timeouts see details of *Instant Teamwork* on page 184.

Weaponry

There's a special class of prop that can broadly be described as weaponry. Once upon a time this was the special province of the school teacher – canes and slippers to punish misbehaviour, blackboard rubbers and books to hurl at the heads of inattentive pupils. Now there's a wider opportunity. Harmless weaponry such as water pistols and soft foam balls can be used by both trainer and trainees. For example, the trainer can use a soft ball to pass control of a discussion. Trainees can be issued with weapons, for instance when members of different groups are giving feedback, to ensure that they keep to time or do not veer off the subject.

Such weaponry has to be used with care. Like any other prop, the purpose is to reinforce the message, not distract from it. But used infrequently with the right timing, weaponry is a great energy booster for trainees, and can bring some highly needed fun into the proceedings.

Bonding

The relationship between trainee and trainer is at the heart of effective training. If it is possible to move from an 'us and them' position to one where both trainees and trainers see themselves as part of the same team, much more can be achieved.

Bar council

Some while ago, as a senior manager of a large company, I attended a three-day residential course – a general management and leadership session. The trainers had been brought in from a different country. They began by attacking a number of things that I held dear. I was determined within three-quarters of an hour that I would resist them and argue at every possible alternative.

This made for a bumpy first day, but in the evening the trainers joined a group of us who had been unhappy with the course at the bar. By the time we all staggered to bed, we were much happier with the whole course and with the presenters in particular. They had ceased to be 'them' and had started to be 'us'. The small differences of international culture had been overwhelmed by our common humanity.

The case study is not a great example of how to do training. Arguably the trainers should not have started out provocatively, and I should not have had a xenophobic instant dislike of them and their course. However, the lesson of the session at the bar is obvious. It is possible, given time, to overcome many potential training problems by building a team rapport between trainers and trainees.

Overcoming 'them and us' does not have to involve alcohol. It can be achieved right at the start by using members of the same group as the trainees to do the training (see *Manager as trainer* on page 78). But in many circumstances the trainer cannot be part of the trainee cohort. Where this is the case, be sensitive to the differences. Don't trample all over the trainees. You need to earn their respect and to move into a team position. And all this without the length of time that is normally available for team building.

A number of factors can influence this process. Make sure there is an intellectual basis for respect – the more trainers actually know their subject (rather than reading it up for the first time the night before), the more likely they are to earn respect. Having some easily recognized marker (an academic title or a book published on the subject) can help here. You can also try to match the educational or socio-economic grouping of the trainees and trainer to encourage early bonding, though this does not guarantee success.

The opportunity for social interaction is very valuable. This is where a residential course comes into its own, as there is so much more time to make bonding happen – especially evenings, which are a more natural time for this. However, practically any course lasting longer than a couple of hours will have opportunities for bonding in the form of coffee breaks, meal times, etc. Even if the course doesn't offer any of these, you can engineer one. Have coffee and tea served at the start of the course. Use that short period as people arrive to start breaking down the barriers.

An essential to make this happen is to give all your effort during the breaks to social interaction. If you are reading your newspaper, or checking your slides and your notes, or if the trainers stay together in an exclusive clique, there will be the opposite effect to that desired. You need to get in among the trainees. Talk to them. Listen to them. Smile at them. It sounds painful, but after a while you can even get to like it.

Making use of the opportunities for bonding that present themselves, and engineering opportunities, will maximize the chance of delivering an effective course.

Manager as trainer

Training offers a wonderful opportunity for a manager to get closer to his or her staff. Residential training, particularly, is excellent for building a team spirit whatever the subject, and if the manager is involved, either as a participant or as a trainer, it can be a very effective way to bring the team together.

The monthly meeting

Although this approach is particularly suited to residential sessions it can also fit well in small chunks as part of a team meeting. When I ran the PC Centre for British Airways, a group of around 30 people who provided all the PC and software purchasing and support for the organization, a regular feature of our group meetings was a short (perhaps 20 minutes) training session that I ran. This might be on a technical subject or customer service issues or cover general business training. This worked well because I was a manager with a technical background – if a non-technical manager attempts technical training of technical staff he or she is asking for trouble.

There is a proviso to this approach. It is a good way to bring the manager and team together if the manager is already seen as a positive part of the team, or at least neutral. If, however, there are problems between the manager and the team, it is best to take explicit team-building action first, as otherwise the manager's presence will simply dampen the enthusiasm of the rest of the attendees without helping team effectiveness. Note that the manager must already have appropriate knowledge – if not, there is a danger that the quality of training will suffer because the manager hasn't got the depth of experience to support the trainees appropriately.

While a good leader will almost always be a natural trainer, you will find that many managers aren't all that good at it. Training will help, but it would also be advantageous if a professional trainer could sit in on a couple of early sessions and give the manager help in developing his or her style.

With these provisos out of the way, from the manager's viewpoint this is a superb move. As we've already seen (page 4), in the real world this is a money-saving step. It promotes teamwork, helps the manager develop communication skills and makes sure that the staff see that the manager is fully behind the training. He or she can also ensure that the training takes the political slant that suits the manager, rather than that of the training department or even senior management in the company.

Don't underestimate this last aspect. If real-world finance says that it's cheaper for a highly paid manager to do the training than a trainer on a lower salary, real-world politics says that everything has a slant. Few presentations, no matter how 'factual', are entirely without bias. There is a wonderful example in Jonathan Lynn and Anthony Jay's *Complete Yes Prime Minister*, where the same (fictional) news story is shown first with a slant that is against the government, then with one that is supportive. Each story can be represented as 'objective' news, yet the feeling is totally different. Similarly, especially when dealing with soft training subjects, a manager may wish to influence his or her staff to have a particular view that is not necessarily the party line.

From the training department's viewpoint, having a manager give training is a mixed blessing. The political slant aspect may go against current thinking. The manager may simply not be a very good trainer. And the approach appears to lessen the influence of the training department (and to threaten trainers' jobs). The only sensible approach to take is to move from a nationalized industry viewpoint to that of a commercial consultancy. The training department should see itself as a commercial operation with expertise to sell – this is, after all, the knowledge economy – rather than the thought police who control how training is to be done. Provided your product is good enough and well enough sold, you should have nothing to fear.

Although the label is 'manager as trainer', in fact any member of staff could provide this type of training. Such an approach is particularly valuable if one member of a team has specialist technical knowledge that you want to spread amongst the team, or if one member of a team is particularly good at picking up information from a book and can then spread it to the rest of the team.

An advantage of this approach that should not be overlooked is that the trainer remains available to the trainees after the course. It's often frustrating when a course has finished to come back to the office and find there is some little point that isn't quite clear, and can't be cleared up with the material supplied. If the trainer is the manager or a member of the team, it's a trivial task to get this follow-up – on demand supplementary training.

4C **VEHICLES**

This is the age of the team. As I've commented elsewhere, you only have to compare the implied weighting of 'she's a teamworker' and 'he's a loner'. Certainly training is an area where group working can be very valuable, but the ritual of breaking into small groups, sharing a task, then feeding back to everyone else has become a painful stereotype. We still need group working, but there have to be ways to make it different and exciting again. From real competitive challenge to group creativity, these sections enhance the group experience.

Whether or not teams are involved, the model for too much training is still the school. The assumption is that the trainer knows it all (even if we are dealing with a professional trainer who is an expert in training, not the subject being trained) and the trainee knows nothing. This can be particularly dangerous when trainees themselves are professionals with a high level of education. For some trainees a more realistic approach is to set a target, give the trainees some tools and let them get on with achieving their goals, using the lessons of what has happened to put across any missing messages. This requires much more flexibility of the trainer, but can be extremely beneficial.

The whole tenor of this book is to turn the elements of training on their head to come at the exercise afresh – never more so than when examining the vehicles of training itself.

Key topic – Target plus toolkit

In an era where we expect more and more independence from our staff, it's strange that most training is tightly structured. It's a bit like giving a chef a ready meal instead of a pile of ingredients – it works for some, but you'll never achieve greatness. An alternative approach is to give the trainees the tools they need to do their own training and let them get on with it within the structure you provide.

Riot in Training Room H

In my early years with a large company I was the most junior trainee on a company training session on effective presentations. The attendees on this course were from the Operational Research department, all highly intelligent people with at least two degrees and a proven track record in dealing with difficult problems. Unfortunately, the trainer dealt with the group like a class of 10-year-olds, sticking rigidly to the lesson plan and labouring each point, virtually clubbing the concepts to death.

Lacking any outlet for their flexibility and energy, the trainees began to take it out on the trainer. While it would be exaggerating to say there was a riot, these were not a happy two days. The trainees were running rings round the trainer, who clearly was not in the same league and could not keep up, nor fend off the questions which varied from mocking to out-and-out verbal attacks.

In the example above, the course content and the trainer were inadequate for the attendees. A high-power group does not want to be led by the nose. In most circumstances such people would rather be given the tools to learn the specific requirements and the space and flexibility to get on with it their way. This does not exclude the value of the trainer, but puts him or her into the role of a facilitator and coach rather than a traditional teacher. It's probably best to illustrate this concept with an example.

Effective presentation revisited

Let's imagine the failed effective presentation course in a target plus toolkit format. The session starts with an introductory talk, no more than an hour. This outlines the objectives of the two days, explains the approach, introduces the toolkit and clarifies the role of the trainer. The days are split into one-hour segments. In the first hour, the attendees are to decide on the approach they want to take, talk it through with the trainer and organize any team working required. In this particular case, the objectives were to learn to give effective presentations and to have the chance to give at least two presentations each.

The attendees decide to brainstorm their immediate views on what makes a good and bad presentation and then undertake some individual research on presentation skills. Mid-afternoon they would then each have five minutes to present their findings back to the group. From the initial brainstorming, each would be given a different aspect of presentation, so that the group would not suffer from the mind-numbing effect of everyone giving a presentation on the same topic. After each presentation there would be three bits of rapid-fire feedback – the individual assessing his or her performance, the rest of the course giving constructive criticism and the trainer summarizing and adding any extra thoughts.

The group decided that on the second day they would finish by midday and take the afternoon off. The morning would start with all of them viewing tapes with segments of good and bad presentations. They would then hold a creativity session on new ways of enhancing presentations. Over an extended coffee break, each member of the team would put together a presentation on an issue that is important to them. Finally, another cycle of presentation and feedback would finish off the day.

There are two particular aspects of this approach that may seem alien initially. The first is giving the trainees so much control over what they are going to do. How this is introduced will depend on the degree of self-determination the trainees are used to. If they are self-starters it can be launched into straight away. If they are used to being led by the hand they will need more help and direction, but can still set their own agenda. Sometimes this will be revolutionary. They may decide to take the session out of the training room. They may decide, as here, to finish early. It is up to the trainer as coach and facilitator to ensure that this aspect is handled sensibly. It's fine to let them finish early, for example, provided there's a check at the end that all the objectives have been met. If they haven't, they should continue. If they have, why not go home? Surely the quality of training is in what is learnt, not how long the trainees spend in the training room?

It may also be the case that the trainer finds the trainees' expectations to be totally unrealistic, or too limited to meet the course objectives. In this case, the trainer should highlight this up front and try to sell the trainees on a change of course. If they are determined to do it their way, let them start, on the understanding that there will be regular reviews every 25 per cent or so of the time through the course. Unless appropriate milestones are met, the course will have to be reshaped. Given this safeguard, why not let them do it their way? After all, mistakes are the most powerful learning tools, and it's just possible that they will know themselves and their capabilities better than you do and will surprise you.

The second worrying concept is the stage where the trainees are let loose to undertake individual research. There are a number of implications. You have to have the right resources available. While this approach to training will actually require less formal preparation from the trainer, it will need a whole raft of resources. In this particular example, apart from the obvious presentation resources from flip charts to presentation graphics software and projector, there will need to be access to the Internet, allowing maybe half of the course to be surfing the Web simultaneously, reference books, sample presentations and videos of good and bad presentations.

The trainer will need to have some experience in researching information, so he or she can help trainees who aren't sure where to begin. The trainer will also have contributed to the distribution of tasks, making sure that there aren't any glaring gaps in the individual briefs. Then it is up to the individual. This will make some trainers uncomfortable. We aren't used to relying on individuals, having been indoctrinated for so long in the HR gospel that teamwork is the only way to go forward. Yet creativity generally stems from the individual, and effective research is usually an individual activity.

There is also the issue of time for research. What if you are dealing with a topic that can't be broken up into chunks that can be researched in (say) an hour and fed back to the other team members in 5 or 10 minutes? In practice, there are few training activities that can't be approached in this way. It may take multiple sessions, but most will adapt to it. After all, we know that training should be chunked with very regular breaks, so the breakdown of the topic should not be a problem. If there simply isn't time to do the research, because you need to read six 500-page books to get the gist of the topic, then part of your preparation will have to be pre-digesting that information into an appropriate form, otherwise your trainees will need to read the books before the course, or, better still, you can provide research guides that help the trainees find their way around the reference sources. Research guides will almost always come in handy. And if a book does take a lot of reading, with a two-day course (as in this example), you might suggest that the researcher takes it home and reads it overnight. Overtime? Maybe, but if the trainee has really been bitten by the topic he or she will want to do it.

When the individuals report back there's a multiple benefit. Instead of all working on the same topic there has been parallel processing, pulling in a whole range of information. The feedback should be more interesting than usual in training sessions, because it isn't just repackaging what the trainer has already said. It's original and each trainee will have a different slant on the topic. And unlike many presentation courses, the content of the presentations will be just as valuable to the course as the practical exercise of giving them.

Don't be tempted to miss out this aspect and simply go for the self-determination. The individual research phase will give much more of a sense of achievement, and research can be fun – it's detective work with the trainee as detective. And of course, they may even come up with something you wouldn't have thought of telling them in the first place.

Creative creativity

I had intended to stick to a single example, but there is one problem with the effective presentation issue – the particular subject is something of a 'common sense' piece of training, the sort of thing anyone might be expected to be able to assemble from scratch. What about technical training or an exercise where even doing the research might require some foreknowledge? I'll use the example of the business creativity training with which I'm most familiar.

Creativity training comes up against a couple of barriers. Until the trainees have seen creativity techniques in action they are unlikely to accept their benefits. And the techniques themselves require some basic introduction before they can be practically used. But that doesn't invalidate the approach. The basics can be put across in a one-hour presentation. That still leaves most of a one- or two-day training course for the trainees to organize themselves, research and act. There may be a short up-front session or a series of mini-tutorials through the course, but after that it can still be left to the trainees to plot their destiny.

This approach to training isn't totally unheard of — it is used by high-performing army groups like the SAS — but it is still relatively uncommon. A large contributory factor to this is that it feels high risk. It's true that there will be more variation in performance, and there is a risk factor, but it should be remembered that it is only the trainees who can ultimately make use of the training, so to put the process into their hands (with the trainer as helper and coach) makes a lot of sense.

Playing games

Learning through play is solidly established as a methodology in primary education, but by the time we reach professional training it has disappeared. Is this a good thing? Perhaps not.

Age of Empires

A couple I know who are educating their son at home can be heard giving him unusual encouragement. Where most parents spend time telling their children to stop playing computer games and get on with their homework, this particular boy is actually encouraged to play certain games – at the time of writing, an adventure game called Age of Empires II, The Age of Kings.

The parents are convinced of the benefits. 'In playing this game, he isn't just having fun, he's learning. Each campaign takes place in a different historical period with plenty of background information that needs to be absorbed if the player is to get on well. Not only does he get this unusually vivid information, he can see practically how battles of the period were fought, what made the difference between success and failure and how key technological developments transformed battle. Of course some of the history is simplified – but less so than by Hollywood, and probably no more so than in a history text for his age group. How many other ways of learning history mean that you have to restrict the time the student spends studying because they are so eager?'

Games (and we aren't talking role play here) don't feature much in professional training. In part it's down to a general business fear of fun. We don't like people to have fun at work. It's somehow too frivolous, unbusinesslike. We are supposed to be sober, sensible people, after all. But when examined closely this premise breaks down. Why shouldn't work be fun? We get more out of it; the company gets more out of it from our improved productivity and creativity (proven accompaniments of enjoying your work). And the same goes for training.

It isn't always possible, and it's sometimes too expensive to be practical, but the combination of games and learning has great potential. If it's possible to make training such fun that people would want to do it in their spare time, the whole concept has changed. This doesn't mean that you necessarily do offer training in people's spare time – though it's worth considering. After all, one of the biggest drawbacks of training is that it takes essential staff out of their line jobs. But implementing such spare-time training generally requires a combination of no coercion to attend and making the activity so enjoyable that most people will want to take part.

There are many ways that games can be used as part of training and development – these are only a few. Look at the kinds of game the target audience likes to play and find ways to adapt them. Sometimes the actual environment of the game can deliver the training without any specific content – for example by playing practically any game, from computer games to board games, in a foreign language to improve language skills.

E-gaming

In the case study a computer adventure game was used as an educational tool, and this particular format lends itself very effectively to learning soft skills. An adventure game is, in effect, like an interactive book. It is a world you can wander round on the screen, interacting with characters and objects around you as the plot unfolds. The players often have to solve puzzles, based in part on information that was gleaned around the electronic world they temporarily inhabit.

The great benefit of the adventure game is that the background story can provide the basic training information, while the puzzles and inter-actions with the characters can test and reinforce that information. A training adventure game could be set in the 'real world' of the training environment – for instance, a game aimed at helping airline check-in staff could be set in an airport – or could use a more traditional adven-ture environment (fantasy, science fiction or historical) with a storyline that incorporates the appropriate training. It's even possible to have multiple trainees in the same adventure, who can interact with human trainers, playing special characters.

Developing such a training game is not cheap, although you can buy adventure-building kits that effectively render the game construction point-and-click. After building the game, though, you have a very cheaply deployed resource.

Adventures aren't the only computer games that lend themselves to training. The other formats discussed below have computer-based equivalents. It is also possible to use a computer game as a direct simulation of some more physical aspects of training. For instance a flight simulator program gives plenty of early experience in piloting skills. Similar simulators could be produced for train and bus drivers, or machinery operators. Another opportunity for game-based learning is in strategy simulations. These simulate an environment, from the old classic SimCity, where the player was a town planner, to business simulations. The opportunity for gaining broad experience and learning about dealing with different scenarios is very high in such games.

While the final popular strand of computer games — those involving movement and destruction — has little impact on training, there remain plenty of possibilities for benefit from the other formats.

Seeking out treasure

The treasure hunt is an ever-popular game, particularly when the game is spread over a large playing area, either using cars or walking. Treasure hunts can be combined with training rather as an adventure game is on a computer — the background information that must be absorbed to be able to solve the clues forms the core of the training. The treasure-hunt format is particularly good as it ensures that the player splits up the learning into small chunks (with driving or walking in between), an essential for maximizing retention. Furthermore, the physical need to get from place to place adds energy to the session. Much cheaper to produce than a computer game, the treasure hunt can provide anything from a quick half-hour introduction to a whole day's activity.

Panels and quizzes

A perennial favourite on the TV are panel games and quizzes. While it's obvious that these can be used to test learning, they can also provide the initial training input. This is especially true with the quiz equivalent of an open examination, providing the players with a good library that will cover all the topics in the quiz. This way, if no one already has expertise in the particular topic, it is possible to read up on it and come up with an answer. Such an approach slows down the pace — but then this is a quiz for the participants, not the audience.

A variant that overlaps into treasure hunting is the approach used on the old TV game show where a 'runner' was directed over a map, by players in the studio who had both the clues and a library of information. This 'panel game treasure hunt' lacks the movement associated with a real treasure hunt, but does enable the players to make more use of reference materials to expand their knowledge.

What about outdoor activities?

The closest training has traditionally come to playing was in the outdoor activity courses, chiefly aimed at team building by putting a group of people through a series of physical challenges. Such courses have acquired a bad reputation, in part because in some instances attendees were forced to attend (or risk losing promotion prospects). A clear example of the lack of regard in which they're held by the general public is the way a UK soap opera storyline recently had several characters sent off on such a course, which was universally hated and mocked by the attendees.

The fact is that orienteering and abseiling and assault courses have lost their gloss. The fun involved is subsumed in the seriousness of the exercise. While many attendees come away with a positive view of the event, there's a strong feeling that this is mostly on a 'I like being hit on the head with a hammer because it's great when it stops' basis. While I know others who still swear by the rugged outdoor event, I think it has had its day and it is time to reinvent the format.

A better model, I would suggest, than the army training that much of the traditional outdoor activities are based around, is the activity adventure TV show, such as *Crystal Maze* and *Fort Boyard*. These shows present teams with a series of challenges combining physical effort and problem solving, using a fantasy format that puts the whole thing into a storyline, rather than being a series of unrelated activities imposed by a sadistic trainer. Because of the richer story-based environment there is much more opportunity for learning above and beyond the elements of teamwork (though teamwork is certainly a major factor), and most importantly there's fun as well as challenge. If you wouldn't normally watch a TV show like this, seek it out in the schedules and watch it with training in mind. Bear in mind that you don't necessarily need the glossy settings – any large disused location is ripe with possibilities.

Books alone

The cost of a day's training is often equivalent to a day's salary or more, without even considering the cost of lost work. There is, however, a low-cost alternative that is used much less often than it should be in the business world – the book.

The true University of these days is a collection of books.

Thomas Carlyle

First some statistics. The average business book costs between one-tenth and one-hundredth of the cost of a day of training. During nearly 20 years working in large companies I was sent on an average of seven days' training a year. I was given three books in the whole period. I still have the books readily accessible, but I can't remember 95 per cent of the training.

There is something crazy going on here. Let's look at the pros and cons of giving training in the form of a book or audio book.

Pros:

- It's cheap – let's not undervalue the benefits of a cheap solution. Forget those impressive statements about how much the company wants to educate its staff. Cheap is the way of the world.
- You are accessing worldwide experts – anyone from a single-person business to a major corporation can call on a top business guru, or find just the right approach to meet their needs.
- There's more opportunity to go into depth – although most business books can be skim-read in a day, they have the room to expand on a topic and give optional side-tracks to explore.
- You don't have to be certain of the application – being cheap has a secondary benefit. When comparing the cost and benefit of training you have to apply a risk factor to the benefit that the output of the training won't be used by the individual. With such a low cost you can afford to take a few relatively high-risk, high-payoff gambles. There may be a subject that might, just might, make a big difference to a particular workgroup. There's much less at stake with a book than with course-based training.

- It's self-paced – we all learn at different rates, in different ways, but all the research suggests we learn best in chunks with breaks. It's much easier to chunk up a book, giving each section the time you want to apply to it, with appropriate breaks in between, than it is conventional training.
- You can use it practically anywhere – a book can be read in the office, on the train, on the loo, in the bath, in bed. Audio books can be listened to in all these places plus the car. The book opens up the whole of life as a training opportunity rather than being forced into a rigid schedule.
- It's a constant reminder – many people hang on to books long after they've read them. A good book may be reread several times. What's more, the book's mere presence on the shelf is a visual reminder of what was learnt.
- It can be company badged – where a large company decides to make use of a book as a training opportunity, it can be given a company-specific cover at little extra cost. This both gives the book a flavour of being part of a corporate initiative and gives you an opportunity to incorporate a company message on the cover.
- It's a present – the element of receiving a gift should not be trivialized. Whenever an employee is given a physical item to keep by their employer it has more of an impact than the equivalent in cash. Money in the bank is an essential, but it is intangible. A present, even one as practical as a book, has a special feel to it.

Cons:

- You can't learn from a book – of course this isn't true, but some people do say it. There's quite an influence from the allegedly Confucian saying 'What I hear, I forget; what I see, I remember; what I do, I understand.' It's certainly true that practical, hands-on experience is often the best skills training, but a book is a great way to get the basics across, and can include plenty of exercises to undertake as you go. What they more often mean is 'I can't motivate myself', which is certainly something that needs to be added to the mix – see *Motivating to learn* in this section.
- They won't actually read it – some won't. But that's often the fault of those giving out the book. There's no reason why you can't combine

giving the book with allocating a small amount of time (perhaps 20 per cent of the time that would have been spent on the course) to reading the book during working hours. Given this push, most staff worth employing will continue with any extra reading needed in their own time.

- There isn't a book that meets our specific needs – this smacks of the 'not invented here' syndrome. There is a fallacy that 'our business' (whatever it is) is so different from everything else that we can only use specific, bespoke training. Of course there are technical tasks (operating the BigCo Left-Handed Treadle Tweaker) that will need totally tailored training, but the vast majority of business training and development isn't like that. If it's just a matter of finding the right flavour, the chances are you can in the millions of books in print. See *Finding your materials* in the support section.

- It's shooting yourself in the foot – this is the most difficult one to handle. The basis is another one of these 'facing the real world' issues. Many trainers will be reluctant to use books as it seems to devalue their role. If you prove that books can be used effectively, why not slash the training budget? I'm not arguing that books could ever replace all of training. The important thing is getting a better balance. You can save costs, and yes, you might lose some training budget, but business these days is about being smart, not necessarily being the one with the biggest budget.

- We've got a library – so why do we need to give out books to individuals? For a start, business people don't use libraries. Gross generalization, but most don't. A book delivered to your desk is there when you've got time for it. A book you've got to stroll down to the library and get is too much trouble, especially if 20 other people want it at the same time. It's just not the same. This approach doesn't replace the library – we're talking about maybe 5 to 10 books per person per year. In fact, if anything, you may find use of the library grows as a book-using culture grows and staff follow up further reading opportunities.

- The trainee gets to keep something we've paid for – this is the other 'real world' snag. It's bizarre, but many companies really don't like their employees getting something that they haven't paid for. It doesn't make sense, but it's often true that there is such a resistance in corporate culture. The fact that the trainee will get significant benefit, and that we're paying much less than we would for a course, seems to be irrelevant. Because a book is tangible (and worse still, might be enjoyed), there's a puritan streak that gets offended. All that can be done about this is to point out how ludicrous such a stance is, and to emphasize the parallel benefits of books.

If a company cut its training budget per head by just 10 per cent and provided books instead, they would be able to provide a much broader training resource. What's more, it would enable them to reach a wider audience. Topics like time management or personal development would be valuable for every employee. You might only be prepared to pay for courses for managers to attend, but the right books can bring them to the whole workforce.

I've encouraged you elsewhere to look deeper into the reasons behind decisions and requirements. Taking such a viewpoint, you ought to see that I have a vested interest in suggesting the use of books. This is true, but unconnected to the argument. I believe that books just aren't used enough in training, and there is too much assumption that it is the responsibility of the individual to pay for business books. They form a potential asset that businesses should not waste.

The humble cassette

We are so used to the impact of new technology that it can be easy to overlook established technology. The audio cassette is still a great way to get information across, especially to a management audience that spends a fair amount of time each day in a car.

His master's voice

At one time in my career I ran the Emerging Technologies group of a corporate. Part of our role was to educate management about new developments in technology. We tried various newsletters and electronic formats with very mixed results. We were getting through well to junior managers, but higher levels of the hierarchy didn't seem to be reading our output.

After an ideas session we realized that senior managers spent more than the average amount of time in the car. They rarely used public transport. Most of them commuted further than the junior staff. And they were more likely to use the car during the day to get from one site to another, or to undertake off-site visits. We made the next newsletter available in an audio tape format. The day after sending it out, we got back detailed feedback from several senior recipients, including a director.

Just think about it in terms of opportunity. The average manager is in his or her car 10 or more hours a week, in and around working time. This is slack time. Wasted time. If you can get your training into this time slot, you have a real advantage.

Consider the use of audio cassettes. These might be bought-in cassettes of books or training courses, or your own material on a tape. If you can find a professionally made cassette, so much the better, but it's not too much of a problem if you can't. Putting together an audio session is less expensive and less technically challenging than video. Provided you put some effort into finding a speaker whose voice comes across well in the medium, and use good-quality recording equipment, you can put together an effective course this way. Bear in mind the matters raised in the topic on public speaking (see *Speaking to the masses*, page 58). You don't want to put your trainees to sleep, especially if they're driving a car. But using a cassette could help you reach an audience that would be totally beyond your reach in any other way.

There's a surprising amount of resistance to this approach because it's old technology. A while ago I was speaking to the New Media editor of a magazine publisher. It was his job to produce exciting new adjuncts to magazines like cover CDs and Web sites. When we'd talked about it, he accepted that the ideal way to get information to his business readers was on an audio tape – but that it would never be used, because it looks too old fashioned, reminiscent of the way computer games magazines used to have cassettes on the covers in the 1980s. There's a barrier to overcome here, but once you are aware of it, it should not be too much of a problem.

Although the training session can be entirely on a tape, which is why the topic appears under delivery vehicles, like *Hollywood or bust* (page 60), it is also possible to use this approach as a reinforcement to a course. Just don't forget the humble cassette.

I want to tell you a story

The story has been the prime teaching tool for 99 per cent of our history, yet it is shamefully ignored in most modern training. It's time to bring back the story with a bang.

Setting the world on fire

'I was working with a group of supervisors from a large printing company in the north of England. Most were in their mid-50s, all had worked with the company for many years, and in most cases had received little or no management training during that time.

'The topic of the day was "leadership and teambuilding", and I must admit we were struggling a bit with the concept, particularly as the group told me (almost proudly) that they believed they had never worked together as a team. "What, *never*?", I asked, hoping to jog someone's memory. They were adamant that such was the culture of the traditional company where they worked that they had never experienced a feeling of team support and cohesion.

'There followed a pregnant, almost defiant silence. Someone cleared his throat. Another folded his arms. My mind was frantically thinking up the next question. And then all of a sudden, Christine, who up to then had volunteered very little, said: "except of course when we had 'the fire'...".

'The rest of the group joined in. "Ah, yes, but that was different, when we had the fire...". The last two words were spoken in almost reverent awe.'

In the ensuing reminiscences, Margaret Parkin, the trainer, noted a series of keywords that amounted to a chapter on management theory. The story of the fire brought out a learning experience that no one would admit without it.

In the mini-case above, there are stories operating at two levels. The story of the fire brought out the learning in the trainees – and the case study is in itself a story. Stories have real advantages over a dry, straight presentation. They are usually more entertaining than teaching. More people are liable to open a novel for a relaxing evening than (say) Duffin's excellent textbook on Electricity and Magnetism, no matter how authoritative the latter or how trashy the former. Let's face it, Jeffrey Archer has sold a lot of books. He might be no great shakes as a novelist (or a politician). His characters may not be well rounded and interesting in an artistic sense. But he understands storytelling.

Stories also get into the mind at a lower level than simple fact. Our brains do not handle knowledge as an encyclopaedia stores information. In the process of learning we generally take an input, make a model of it and fit it into our (largely image-based) chains of memory and association. The model-making part of the process is inevitable. We can't store all there is to know about anything − not even a simple object like a coin. Instead we have a mental model of what it is (it's metal, sort of brassy-brown, weighs about so much, is round and flat, has a face on one side and a picture on the other, has a particular value, good for tossing, hurts if it hits you on the ear) that is in no sense what it *actually* is. In a sense it's a form of story, though a very stream-of-consciousness, James Joyce sort of story. It's not surprising, then, that stories stick, especially when they involve extreme or fantastic images (it's no coincidence that there are so many talking animals in traditional, orally spread stories), which help fix the content in memory.

In fact, the oral tradition has always used stories not just to entertain but as a teaching aid. You've only got to look at the Bible, where Jesus is constantly using parables − stories with a point − in teaching. These come in two forms. One type is the true parable, an illustrative story making a specific point. The story of the good Samaritan, where an unexpected benefactor helps the man in need, is a good example. The other type is the allegory, where each element of the story represents something. So, in a story where seed is cast on stony ground, a patch of thistles and so forth, the seed, the sower, and the different types of ground are each taken to represent something. The first is closer to a metaphor ('selling shares on the Internet is just like having a market stall') − a very effective technique for developing understanding. The second, the allegory, is less immediately obvious, but when absorbed provides a memory chain to handle a more complex set of information.

In essence, the power of the story is to put information in terms that are more approachable and digestible than bare facts. By linking directly into the structures of memory, a story can generate more associations, making the lesson more generally applicable and easier to remember in a wider range of circumstances. And we should never forget the way a story can make learning more entertaining. It's time we got over the Victorian feeling that education has to hurt, and that making learning enjoyable trivializes it.

In business there is a form of story that has particular value – in fact it was used in the case study above – it's the war story: the story from experience that has a lesson for us. Ms Parkin refers to these as 'myths', but the term has too many inappropriate associations and I think that in a business training context, 'war stories' is a more appropriate term. It tells a tale of an encounter in the business, preferably one with a dramatic outcome, that can be used to make a point. This book is littered with them – most of the mini-cases are stories. The illustrative power is obvious. We like to hear about other people and what they have done – it's the attraction of everything from biographies to soap operas. It's why also I find the best business books for a broad education are the 'business biographies' like Wallace and Erickson's *Hard Drive* about Bill Gates, or Ricardo Semler's remarkable *Maverick!* about his own experience (see Appendix, page 183 for more details).

I have a little story of my own to illustrate how powerful such books could be. I was asked by the online bookshop Amazon to write a short piece on my three favourite books of the millennium as part of their year 2000 publicity. Because I write business books I wanted at least one of these to be a business title. But when I came down to it, it was very difficult to find any business book, however much it had influenced me, or however great the theories and techniques, that I could define as one of my favourite books. Then it struck me that I could include business biographies, and Semler's book demanded my attention. (In case you are wondering, the other two were Alan Garner's masterly young-adult fantasy *The Owl Service*, and Gene Wolfe's *There Are Doors*.)

There's a limit to how much I can wax lyrical on the benefits of story-telling in training and learning here – see page 184 for more details of Margaret Parkin's *Tales for Trainers*.

Role play revisited

Role play is a very powerful technique, yet it suffers from a real problem – many trainees hate it. They might appreciate the outcome, but the anticipation of taking part is so bad that some may even drop out of a course if they know there's going to be role play in it.

The spring role

I have to confess that I am an awful person to have taking part in a role play. My creativity training is specifically designed to find ways to cheat assumptions and create new alternative solutions. The trouble is, the role play's designer may not have had these ideas in mind, and so it's all too easy for me to push a role play off the rails. Sadly I have been kicked out of a number of role plays for this creative behaviour.

A good example would be a corporate session that was training managers how to deal with difficult staff. I was playing a team leader. According to the role play, the company had arranged an activity weekend with assault courses and abseiling to improve teamwork. One of my key team members was refusing to attend as she was a regular churchgoer and didn't want to attend a course on a Sunday. (The role play designer had obviously been watching *Chariots of Fire*.) I had to sort things out.

I asked the team member why she didn't want to go. 'Okay', I said, 'you don't have to go'. The trainer was horrified. 'You can't do that', he said. 'Yes I can', I said, 'I just did'. My argument was that in a real situation, I would always consider an individual's right to use their spare time as they chose to have priority over the company's demands on that time. But, argued the trainer, that isn't the point of the exercise. I was applying the rules of the real world and using them to cheat the meta-rules of the role play. 'Let's assume', said the trainer, 'that for whatever reason, everyone must attend or everyone will lose their jobs'. I nodded. New rule taken on board. 'Okay', I said to my patient team member, 'we'll move the course away from the weekend'.

Once more the trainer intervened. 'You can't do that!' I looked at the brief. 'It doesn't say you can't.' The trainer was losing his temper. 'Well, you can't.' And so it went on. He threw in three or four more rules and each time I solved the problem with a solution he didn't like. In the end he gave up. Either his role play or my determination to come up with a creative solution had wasted all our time. I'll leave it up to you to judge which was the case.

There is no doubt that role play will continue to be a powerful technique, but if we are to make the most of it, we will either have to modify the approach to role play or tackle the main points of resistance.

Alternative formats

It is possible in some circumstances to give role play a fresh feel by changing the format or context of the training. One hook to hang this on could be the popularity of improvisational humour games on TV. From the straight improvisational acting through to popular panel games that are nominally quizzes on the news or sport or pop music, these programmes allow performers and personalities to demonstrate their ability to give a spontaneous response to a question that is entertaining to the audience. Where it could be made to fit the training requirement, using a format like this as a vehicle for role play may seem more acceptable than a conventional approach.

Look for other vehicles that could be used to present role play in a way that makes it seem less uncomfortable and more enjoyable.

It's childish

A common reaction is that role play is childish. This is liable to be more of a problem for those who feel they are grown-up and so are less likely to play for the sheer enjoyment of it. A surprising number of adults do still feel themselves a child inside (it's often suggested more of these are men) – this means that they are still happy with toys and probably role play.

The point of the objection from those who find role play childish is that it is not doing a 'real' piece of work. It is frivolous and involves messing about. If you are a busy person who has had to make a real effort to find the time to attend training, it could be that you have a problem with role play because of this.

A useful technique in discouraging this problem is to dispense with the term role play entirely (this is, after all, jargon, which rarely contributes to successful communication). The term is uncomfortably redolent of airy-fairy, social worker, human resources, detachment from reality. (Apologies if you fall into any of these brackets, but like it or not, it is the knit-your-own-yoghurt association that springs up all too easily from this sort of jargon.)

Instead, introduce the approach by saying that experience has shown that this is a skill that is best learnt by practice as well as theory. Ideally you would undertake the real exercise that this approach will simulate, but for whatever reason (make sure there is a reason, otherwise, why don't you do it for real?) you will have use this next-best approach. With the facilities and time you've got you will try to make it as much as possible like the real thing.

If it's labelled anything, a term like simulation has a more neutral feel – but it is quite possible to do without a label entirely.

It's embarrassing

In undertaking a role play it's easy to suffer from stage fright, for just the same reasons as butterflies in the stomach can strike when you go on stage in a play – because you don't want to mess up in front of other people. The more of an audience there is, the worse the sensation. This concern can be tempered by, as much as possible, undertaking the role play in a private location – not in a room with 20 other people undertaking the exercise, and certainly not on a stage with an audience (unless, of course, the point of the role play is to see how well you perform in front of other people).

Reducing the numbers of onlookers can help, but doesn't entirely eliminate the sense of embarrassment. After all, most role plays involve others, who might be taking on a part themselves, but will still be witnesses to your failure should things go wrong. It can help if participants are showing obvious signs of embarrassment to take a couple of minutes time out to discuss how they feel – once shared, the fact that everyone finds it embarrassing will help decrease pressure on individuals.

It's too artificial

A role play is often restricted. In fact, to all intents and purposes they are always restricted. Often you are fitting a process that should take much longer into a short time. Often the physical circumstances are quite different from the situation you are simulating. This is one kind of artificiality that will occasionally cause trouble. That's a minor problem that can usually be overcome by explaining the restrictions of the environment and the session and making sure that the trainees understand that nothing significant is being lost in the mapping onto the more confined circumstances. But that's not the only problem of artificiality.

The one that has always caused me problems when I have been involved with role plays, as illustrated in the case study, is the short-sighted view that was taken when the role play was designed. Most role plays involve decision making and problem solving. A fundamental realization when beginning to take a creative approach is that there isn't a single right answer to practically any question. In fact a large part of creativity training involves undoing the damage done by traditional education, which is inevitably focused on giving *the* right answer – the one expected by the examiner. The world is a much less well-specified place.

There's a real danger in running a role play that you are in school-teacher mode. There is only one right answer – the one you want. Inevitably someone will come across some aspect of the role play that enables them to legitimately come to a different conclusion. It's very tempting to try to steer the role play back to the answer you want. But the result is disastrous. The participant who has hit on an alternative approach will be frustrated. The other participants will either share that individual's frustration, or will grow increasingly irritated with the delay caused by argument. Wherever possible, incorporate the alternative solution into the role play – don't try to undo it.

There is one case, however, where you may have to take some corrective action. Cheating is a classic creative act. Not in the sense of doing someone down, but by discarding the assumptions that everyone else is making. It's how practically every new business succeeds. It's how anyone with any sense copes with a bureaucracy – not breaking the rules, but interpreting them to suit yourself. Many intelligent players will take this approach with a role play. They will try to get to the desired result by making use of the fact that the role play's restricted world is much easier to cheat than the real one. That's fine if the cheating itself can be the primary lesson. Often, though, the cheat is only possible because of the limitation of the role play (see the case study above for an example). In such circumstances, the best approach is to expand the detail of the role play to eliminate the cheat if possible. If this isn't practical it will be necessary to take the cheater to one side and attempt to win him or her over or, in the extreme, to abandon the role play.

This may seem excessive, but once someone has found a way to cheat within the framework of the role play it is very difficult to refocus on the desired lesson. Any attempt to do so seems painfully artificial. It may be better to abandon the exercise for this session and come back to it another time when it has been redesigned more tightly.

This is a problem that can to some degree be prevented by good design. Get several people to think through the design of the role play, looking for such danger spots. Make sure you get very different people involved, with different viewpoints. If you can involve someone with creativity training, even better. You will never design every weak spot out of a role play, but by putting appropriate effort in you can minimize the impact of the unexpected.

It's too heavy handed

This is a special case of the previous problem. A very tempting artificiality is to be heavy handed with the message. After all, the point of the role play is to put across some learning, so the more we can cram into the session the better. Or, perhaps not. We are very sensitive to stories with a message that try to put one over on us. It's fine for there to be a message – but it has to come across naturally. By all means make a point in your role play, but don't put it across in a way that five-year-olds would find irritatingly obvious. Aim the material at your trainees' age, not their shoe size.

Breakout groups overhauled

The breakout group is a natural enough component of training in groups. But this is probably the most hackneyed vehicle in the training repertoire, leaving it in serious need of overhaul.

Yawn central

We've all been there. The training session breaks into groups, each of which is to put together a short presentation on their thoughts on a topic. The first group gives what seems to the trainer quite an interesting presentation (at least one person in each of the other groups doesn't notice; he or she is much to busy desperately trying to work out what to say). The second presenter stands up. 'We pretty much came up with the same things.' The trainer has seen this before (all too often). 'Why don't you just tell us what's different', she says. The second presenter either tries to do this, totally ruining his team's presentation because he's having to rewrite it as he goes, or (more likely) ignores the request and ploughs through all the same stuff again.

And so it goes on. After five, short, mind-numbingly boring presentations, everyone is in dire need of a visit to the bar. Each presenter is determined to show that they have produced a reasonable amount of output, and displays it despite any common-sense requirement to pick out the highlights that make his or her team's thinking different. And can you blame them? After an hour's hard work and acrimonious arguing, would you like to stand up and say 'actually we've nothing original to say' to the audience and quite possibly your boss?

Something has to change, yet there is good reason for keeping the breakout group. Discussion in groups over around seven in size is wasteful of time and suppressing of creativity. To get any sense of movement, to involve everyone in an exercise, it is necessary to break down into small groups. But how can this be achieved to make the most of the groups and to collect the results without producing boredom? It's not an easy premise, but here are a few suggestions.

Non-parallel strands

As the problems with breakout groups come back to repetition, the simplest solution is to have non-parallel strands, with each group considering a different aspect of the topic. This has the advantage of removing the repetition, but there are some dangers too. Some people are unhappy with taking the input of others, needing to be actively involved in the process. Sometimes you will have a group that simply lacks the effectiveness to come up with anything worthwhile.

The deciding factor on parallel strands is how much you are aiming for an 80 per cent solution. If the intention is to cover as much as possible, parallel strands are essential to maximize the spread of input. If, however, you decide that it is enough to get a reasonable set of thoughts, there is nothing wrong with non-parallel strands. It all comes down to how pragmatic the training is going to be. No one is going to take away 100 per cent of your training as absorbed knowledge. Whether or not you are happy with non-parallel strands will depend to some extent on your acceptance of this.

Technique separation

The output of breakout groups can be strongly influenced by the techniques used in the group. If each group is approaching the same topic but using a totally different technique, it is possible to improve the spread of results and hence reduce the boredom of feedback. For instance, if the groups were discussing 'what makes a good brand' in training on branding, each group could use a different creativity technique (see page 140 for more on creativity techniques) to generate ideas. With this approach, rather than the traditional uniform brainstorming, a wider spread of thoughts will be developed.

Alternatively, each group could take a particular aspect of the topic. For instance, if the subject was customer service, one team could list what makes for good customer service, one what makes for bad customer service, one could list extra things the company could do and another could list activities the company could stop doing... or whatever. The important point is to widen the techniques used in the groups.

Edited highlights

Feedback from breakout groups to the whole course can be valuable. The individual groups will have their own insights, which it is useful to share. However, this inevitably leads to the problem of overlap and feedback fatigue. To get round this, there is a lot to be said for taking an approach that combines the feedback.

There are a number of methods that could be used. If reporting is required immediately after the breakout sessions, one individual could be charged with moving from group to group, collating output for a single presentation back. Alternatively, each group could have one member elected as go-between, whose job it would be to add each new output to a central board or flip chart. For this approach, a mind map would be a good way of representing the information.

If there is a break available before feedback (not a bad idea, as it's always worth having a short break after a concentrated session of output), a meta-team with a member from each group could pull together the output into a single presentation or mind map. Whichever approach is taken, though, the result is that the whole course is finally taken through a unified picture of the output without overlap and with minimized boredom.

Feedback spectrum

If the breakout groups are still to give individual feedback, something has to be done to make that feedback more interesting. Although the edited highlights approach described above is often attractive, there are circumstances when it is valuable for each group to feed back, even if the information has strong overlaps. If this is the case, it makes sense to reduce the dullness of the process by reducing overlaps elsewhere – for example in the style of the feedback.

Try having a series of cards, each describing a mode of feedback. Shuffle and deal out one card to each breakout group. They are to present their feedback in this manner. The variety of approach will carry the audience over the overlap of content (as long as the sessions aren't too long). Some possible modes are listed below. There are plenty more, depending on the inclination and skills of the members of the team:

- monologue – one person gives a dramatic and/or funny monologue covering the information;
- playlet – the message is put across in a short drama. It is recommended that humour is left to natural ineptitude – acting humour is notoriously difficult;
- video – as the playlet, but on video;
- a straight presentation;
- a talked-through mind map;
- mime – only practically applicable in some softer subjects;
- unison voices – all members of team read the feedback at the same time;
- word split – the members of the team take turns to read a word of the feedback;
- poster design;
- a song;
- graffiti – preferably using a wall and spray cans;
- puppet show;

... and so on.

Action learning

Action learning is a borderline *Training+* activity. It's well established enough to be considered part of the training mainstream, yet it's still interesting enough to need a little more exposure.

There can be no learning without action and no action without learning.

Reg Revans, deviser of action learning

Action learning is one of those subjects that will always split the observers. To some it's the greatest step forward in the development of training. To others it is a collection of platitudes in search of a home. It's certainly true that the quote above veers towards the latter. Not only is it untrue (every atom in the universe is in action; there's no sign of individual atoms learning anything), it is has a classic hallmark of generality – you can substitute various words without invalidating it. Try replacing 'learning' with 'energy' or 'politics', for instance. However, it would be foolish to dismiss action learning for its obvious flaws. The emphasis on action merits consideration.

In brief (see Professor Revan's *The ABC of Action Learning*, page 184, for more detail) action learning posits that there are two components of learning, programmed knowledge – that is, what you can be taught – and questioning insight – the learning that arises from doing. Questioning insight is seen as the prime vehicle for management learning, and the only way to address open-ended problems, as opposed to those with a specific solution.

Instead of employing teaching, action learning involves participants in active work on problems and opportunities (not necessarily their own), aided by a 'set' – in normal language a support group of other active learners. The core of action learning is getting managers to start acting (instead of talking about acting) and to learn from that action – it's an iterative development not unlike prototyping a new product.

Most of the structure of action learning is conventional project management discipline, with a small element of research and learning incorporated into it. This is inevitably an oversimplification, but the point to note is that it is not fearsome, nor is it abstruse. Instead it is a matter of taking conventional management decisions, but actually learning from the process, rather than carrying on in the same old well-worn track.

Action learning does not have to be exclusive. While the experience-driven learning it gives is extremely valuable, it is best accompanied by the broadening influence of the taught learning process, otherwise it is liable to be too inward-looking – a fact that is echoed by the 'old school' origins of action learning. Even so, it should not be ignored. It is a valuable tool if the philosophical baggage is not allowed to take over.

Surprise packages

There are times when the old training adage of telling them what you're going to say, then saying it, then telling them what you said is just too predictable. A great vehicle for moving to *Training+* is the surprise.

The Friday afternoon cure

'I was once involved in a long-term training course which took place on two days, Thursday and Friday each week. The Friday afternoon session was, of course, a nightmare. Not only had the attendees got post-lunch snooze syndrome, they really wanted to go home, and not be on a course at all. The course was about facilitation. We saved the liveliest bit, all the practical facilitation exercises, until that last afternoon to keep them on the ball, but they were still losing it.

'After a couple of weeks we thought we'd try something different. We rewrote the afternoon session. There were still the same number of exercises, giving each attendee a couple of chances to facilitate, some running warm-ups, others doing pure facilitation or something stranger. We told them what they were going to be doing up front, but not who would be doing what when. Through the afternoon, unpredictable slides in the presentation would carry a splash marker and a number. This wasn't in the handouts, and signalled that it was time for the holder of that number to do an exercise. It worked brilliantly, keeping the energy going all afternoon.'

Paul Birch, creativity trainer and author

There is a certain predictability about most training. It follows a set routine. It's rather like a play that has been running for a while in a theatre. It will settle down to working a particular way, and the approach is constant and predictable to a student of the particular author (or trainer in this instance). As I mentioned in the introduction, it's drummed into us to tell them what we're going to tell them, then tell them it, then tell them what we've just told them.

On the whole this is a good thing, certainly for retention, but inevitably by the time you've heard it a third time it has all become a little boring. Of course it's down to the trainer to make sure this doesn't happen – that the three iterations are sufficiently different that they influence retention without seeming repetitious. But even so there are times when an element of surprise can make all the difference.

Think of a novel or TV drama. It's not the stuff that has been flagged up well in advance and comes as no surprise that grabs you by the scruff of the neck and opens your eyes wide. It's not the expected that you discuss the next day at work. It's the shock, the sudden unexpected occurrence. Arguably, surprise in some form is at the heart of all drama. And surprise can help in training too.

By all means have your training session carefully planned. After all, the surprise twist in a play is no surprise to the actors involved – but to the audience, in your case your trainees, it can be the highlight of the event. Having said this, it's perfectly possible to include an element of chance that even you aren't in control of. You could have a course in six different segments and use a die (or the electronic equivalent, which could deal more easily with the reducing number of options) to decide which to undertake next. You could have a range of techniques to use on cards and only decide which to pursue by shuffling and dealing them. At one level, surprise could be an element of chance.

Alternatively, the surprise could come in the form of an unexpected guest – a part of the training session that wasn't previously flagged up to the trainees. Ideally this should be something high energy and interesting, so that it's the sort of unexpected guest that you welcome rather than the sort that makes you hide behind the sofa. This could even extend to a total replacement of a session. 'You thought that this afternoon would be spent studying the voltage differentials on a black box flight recorder…' (yawns from the trainees) 'but in fact we're going up in a plane so you can make direct observations at 30,000 feet.' (Yawns become gapes.)

The element of surprise has a number of valuable contributions to make. It can inject energy, add interest and remove boring predictability. This can be overdone. If the trainees are inexperienced or in an unfamiliar environment, then stability may well be more important – but where the trainees are comfortable, they need something to separate comfort from drowsiness.

Don't forget the form of surprise used in the case study. This is a relatively small level of surprise, so can be used with less secure trainees.

Here the session is fully mapped out, but it is not clear until the appropriate moment which group will be doing their part when, or exactly which of a number of options a group or individual will perform. Like many of the *Training+* topics, this is a mix and match one, where the element of surprise can be incorporated in a wide range of ways to match the requirements of your audience. Be prepared. Be structured. But never forget the value of surprise.

4D SUPPORT

Probably the greatest missed training opportunity is what the trainee is sent away with. There is a great need for support material to get the trainee over the barrier between the artificial training environment and the real world. The memory and the warm glow of a (good) training session will fade all too fast without reinforcement. Yet what do we usually do – give them a ring binder of photocopied handouts to put on the shelf. When it comes to being given 'toys' we are at our most child-like, suspending much adult cynicism. Training has to make more use of prizes and giveaways, and should move as much as possible to using more attractive written materials, like books, rather than A4 sheets. This section looks at the opportunities and pitfalls.

Given any support materials, there is also a need to make sure something is done with them. It has long been understood how valuable it is to reinforce learning by quick revisits after the initial input – but very little business training takes this into account. The training is finished now – it's back to the grindstone. Sections in *Support* look at the opportunities for after-event reinforcement, a particularly rich opportunity to use new media and e-mail as well as conventional means.

Key topic – Books

The six months after a piece of training are the crucial ones. If the trainee has done nothing with the output of the course by then, he or she might as well have not attended.

Visit the shelves

Sit in your work chair. Take a notepad, and note down the last three pieces of training (or developmental courses) you were involved in as a trainee. (Haven't been involved in any? How can you expect to sort out training if you don't experience it?) Now lay your hands on any books, materials and other memory joggers from the courses. Don't do anything with them, just locate them.

This little exercise is well worth undertaking. Often it turns out that you have real problems remembering the last three pieces of training you undertook. Not a good start. If the main refreshment material you have is a set of course notes, the chances are it's filed away somewhere, or with a great pile of other unidentifiable documents somewhere on a shelf. If you got a real book with a course, it might prove a little easier. The book may well be on a clear shelf, easily identified and referred to.

Of course, it doesn't have to be like that. Just getting a book doesn't mean the course (or the book) is any good. But it does seem likely that a course built around a book will have more retention, because a book is a more lasting reminder of the content. There are a number of reasons underlying this. A book is more professional-looking, more compact, feels more pleasant to handle and is easier to refer to at a moment's notice.

This topic isn't about using books as a learning tool in isolation (see page 91). But there are few better support products for anything from a lunchtime session to a major course. Books don't add hugely to the cost of the training – typically £5–15 a head – but the benefits mean that having either a course that is built around a book, or a book as an adjunct to a course, is extremely valuable, a consideration that should be made both in course design and when selecting suppliers for new courses.

I have to put my hands up at this point and revisit my vested interest. As a writer I am hardly likely to discourage people from building books into their training – yet this is an opinion I held long before I started writing, during over a decade as a corporate manager. Look at the post-event sequence of events and compare a book and a typical photocopied handout.

Table 4.1

	Book	Handout
Look and feel on receipt.	Glossy, professional, compact, solid.	Inevitably less slick, large format, tends to fall apart.
Temptation on the way home/at home/ immediately when back at work.	Peek into and see what's different to the course/ whether or not it's interesting.	Stick it the briefcase. Leave it there, or put it on a shelf with the others.
On return to office.	Show colleagues smart-looking book. Others thumb through it.	Leave it on the shelf. Who wants to see another handout?
During the first fortnight.	If the book was interesting (big 'if') read the book: topic reviewed, and revisited with different slant.	Leave it on the shelf.
Long-term storage.	On bookshelf with clearly labelled spine.	In a pile somewhere (or possibly binned).
When a relevant application occurs.	Quick look up in the index and apply.	Probably forget notes exist, but if remember, try to find the notes. Probably don't, but if do, flip through them trying to find something relevant.

The portrayal there might be a trifle extreme, but the message isn't. A single bookshelf could hold the concentrated output of a lifetime's attendance of courses (though hopefully most of us acquire rather more books than this), making an instant library to remind and refresh the attendee. By comparison no other printed material will have the same impact.

A final note – it's not enough to say that there's a copy of the book in the learning centre. This is quite as much a failure as a handout. The psychological impact of the book as a part of the course material is that it's a present. It's something nice that you have been given. Immediately there's a lift. It's yours to do with as you wish. It's there when you need it. It's a constant reminder – not something you have to go down to the business library and hunt out. Suddenly all the advantage has gone away. Training that makes use of a book as an application tool has to make an individual copy of the book available to each trainee.

I can remember now every course I've been on where the principal course material was in the form of a book. In one case (Edward de Bono), the author was giving a course, and there was a double boost out of that, but even with the others – for instance a management course around 15 years ago that included a copy of Tom Peters' *A Passion for Excellence* – the course sticks with me more, and the book is still on the shelf within a metre of my desk. Get books into your courses – it's as simple as that.

E-mail extensions

Everyone agrees that to get the best retention and application after training there should be reinforcement after the course, but how do you do that, especially if your trainees could be dispersed around the world? E-mail offers a new possibility.

E-mail rules

E-mail is now the communication medium of choice if immediacy of receipt is not required. E-mail establishes closure from your end in that you can fire one off as soon as you have established the need to communicate. E-mail is also a very broad vehicle of communication as it can include documents and other computer files as attachments. E-mails can be sent quickly, cheaply and efficiently to a large number of correspondents at once. And they have worldwide scope from a local connection.

Brian Martin, PC Week *magazine*

A lot of misleading remarks have been made about e-mails. They are accused of being dangerous, because they are too easy to fire off without thought. It is pointed out that they come a distant third in the communication stakes after face-to-face and letters. This misses the point. E-mail is immensely valuable *because* it is so easy to fire one off. An e-mail is much more likely to get sent than a letter, and even more likely than arranging face-to-face meetings with remote contacts on a regular basis. E-mail may not be the richest communication vehicle, but an actual e-mail is worth a lot more than a letter that never gets sent or a meeting that is never arranged.

For the purposes of reinforcing a training session the same arguments apply. It would be ideal if you could talk to all the people, but will it happen? It would be more personal if you sent a hand-written letter to each attendee, but are you going to? If you do contact trainees and ask for feedback, which is more likely to get it, an e-mail where the trainee just has to press the reply button or a letter that requires them to write their own letter, address it and post it? The great thing about e-mail is that you can use it in a big way – not just a tentative 'how did it go' follow-up, but a full programme of reinforcement.

It might go something like this:

- Next day – send a 'thank-you' message reinforcing one key point and acquainting attendees with the reinforcement programme. In the same e-mail give a contact e-mail address in case they have any subsequent queries about anything learnt on the course. This is a two-way process. You are setting up a customer service relationship.
- After a week – send a document of supplementary information. In the e-mail list a handful of Web sites with further information relevant to the course, and half a dozen books (don't just give their titles, include the URL of an online bookshop like Amazon, so the trainees can order them). Also include a short exercise that will reinforce a key point.
- After a month – send a short questionnaire asking what has stuck, what hasn't and why.
- A week later – follow up the questionnaire, reinforcing the areas of weakness.
- ... and so on.

When does it stop? When it feels right. It might be after a single e-mail, it might be after a year. A useful associated approach is to use e-mail discussion lists, or bulletin boards like Lotus Notes to allow the trainees to discuss the topic interactively. A discussion list is a simple facility that lets all involved e-mail a special central address. This automatically distributes their e-mails to the other members on the list. The list can be moderated (that is, you get a chance to monitor or modify the submissions before they go out), or not. Such list facilities are freely available via the Internet and have the big advantage of being accessible wherever the trainees are based.

A bulletin board (also known as a newsgroup) provides more structure than a discussion list. Members can place an e-mail on the board, other contributors can then reply to it and the result builds up as a 'threaded' discussion, where messages and their replies are structured together in a tree. Whether a discussion list or a bulletin board is provided, it can be used by both the trainers and the trainees to share information and experiences – in fact trainee-to-trainee communication is amongst the most valuable, as the trainees can learn from each other's mistakes.

What if there are attendees on the course who don't have e-mail? Presumably this means making special arrangements to reach them with ordinary letters? Or perhaps not. You would achieve a lot more by making sure that they did get on e-mail, either in the company or at home. Don't give the technophobes and conservatives an easy way out. It's for their own good, and not just in terms of training. Being without e-mail in a 21st-century business is like being without the telephone in the previous century. It's not an option.

Intranet reinforcement

Intranets, using World Wide Web technology but on an in-house network, offer significant opportunities to back up and extend the training regime.

Mining the Internet

In fact, this example is of a case using the Internet, but the approach is exactly the same as a company might take on an intranet. The book *Mining the Internet* has a Web site that is used to extend the learning that the book itself provides. This is done in a number of ways. There are articles that could not go in the book at the time of writing. There are live examples, tied to pages in the book, so that the reader can follow up examples at a click without needing to type in a Web address. There is an e-mail list, which readers can join to get updates sent by e-mail. And there is a corrections section, where errors that readers and others have spotted can be flagged up. The site very much extends the book into cyberspace. Similarly, an intranet site can extend your training onto the desktop, and from there to anywhere that the Internet and the wider Web can carry it.

Let's come back for a moment to the purpose of support. The aim is to extend the training back into the workplace, to reinforce the message, to increase the chances of the training being actually used and to expand on subjects that can't be covered adequately in a training session. An intranet is a great way of providing all of these requirements.

Assuming the trainees work at a desk, the company's intranet is usually available at the desktop. If the trainees aren't office workers there are increasingly often public terminals throughout companies to deliver the intranet to all the workers – after all, the purpose of the intranet is to be an in-house communication vehicle, and this warrants the widest access. This means that any material is available almost instantly, right in the heart of the workplace.

Web technology is also ideal for giving the opportunity for further reading, expansion and digression. The intranet can cover the course, but have jumping-off points along the way that expand on areas of interest. And if the company intranet is set up properly, those jumping-off points can even make use of the whole World Wide Web, not just your intranet's content, to back up your course.

Simply bringing the information to the desktop enhances the chances of it being used, but there can be more. You can have interactive reminders that bring the trainees back to the material at the sort of intervals recommended for best retention. You can tie the training into diaries and project management, making it easy to pick up on a newly learnt technique when it's most likely to be needed. Or you can just make it easy to ask 'how do I ...?' – so often, a few weeks after training it's all hazy enough to need a bit of a pointer.

As far as content goes, everything that was said on Web training (see page 36) applies equally here. Online learning may not be the answer to every requirement, but it's almost always a great backup resource that brings the training back in an instant. The question you should be asking is not 'Should a course have follow-up support material on the intranet?' but 'Is there a reason why this course shouldn't have follow-up support material on the intranet?' The default assumption should be that the resources will be there.

Prizes

We are at our most childlike when being rewarded and given incentives. However childish it may seem, there is nowhere near enough use made of prizes in training.

The booby prize

Generally prizes make superb motivational elements, but be very clear exactly what it is that you are giving, or an expensive titbit can become an embarrassing nightmare. At a manager's conference in the early nineties, designed to combine team building and education, the final session opened with a prize draw. 'And here's the prize,' said the presenter. The smoke rose up. The music swelled. A car crashed through the main screen into the auditorium. A gasp went through the audience. They were thrilled.

A few moments later, the prize winner was announced. He went up to collect his prize, the keys of a brand new car. The presenter welcomed him onto the stage. 'And here to give you the keys is a senior executive of rental car firm X, who will loan you this wonderful car free of charge for a whole year.' The audience slumped. Arguably the mood of the whole conference was ruined. An excellent prize – a year's free car hire – had become a negative factor because of mismanagement of expectations. If you expect nothing, a year's car hire is wonderful. If you expect to be given a car, a year's hire is pathetic.

When putting together a piece of training it helps to consider a mental energy level graph of the trainees. A session often starts low-energy owing to uncertainty or post-meal blood distribution. It will then climb to a peak, but before long it is drifting down again. This is partly combated by breaks and the use of warm-ups and timeouts, but prizes also act as an attention grabber. I've seen very well paid people who were paying very little attention to a session suddenly move to full concentration when they heard that there would be an opportunity in the next few minutes to win the latest computer game. The trick is to tie the prize in with a serious piece of learning, so that the carrot achieves a positive result.

Of course, the nature of the prize is important. For simple budgetary reasons you cannot afford to be too generous. In fact a very effective prize can be quite trivial if there is competition for it. But the prize needs to have something about it that will capture the trainees' imagination. What generally proves effective is to start with a trivial prize, as the impact of giving a prize at all will initially be enough. Through the day increase the value of the prize (that's value to the recipient, of course, not necessarily financial value). You might occasionally dip back into lower values, though, especially with something like our first category in the prize chain, sweeties.

Sweeties

The simplest approach to prizes is to get hold of a bag of sweets. They need to be in an individually wrapped form – either single sweets or the small 'treat-sized' boxes. Making sure that you aren't training a team of diabetics (sugar-free sweets are available, though), sweets make an excellent quick prize. They're cheap, attractive in a silly way (one of the hallmarks of a good training prize) and they provide a small physiological boost too, by giving the recipient a hit of sugar that provides near-immediate energy. Although you can initially award sweets as prizes to individuals it's not a bad idea to make sure everyone has access to some soon.

Paperclips

This could be literally paperclips or some other small value, useful item. I've successfully used paperclips for a long time, but with a little twist – they're an unusual design, flat metal clips with the word 'Imagination' printed on them. It's fine to use something as everyday as a paperclip, but make sure that there's something different, something special about them.

In using the paperclips, a big build-up helps. Say that there is going to be an amazing prize. Undertake the exercise. Then, perhaps, admit to lying about the prize. It's a packet of paperclips – but they're very special paperclips. Give a quick spiel about them, so they sound more interesting than paperclips – after the initial shock of what they are, this will go down well. I also sometimes throw in a remark about one residential session where the attendees thought I was giving out condoms (the paperclips come in a rectangular plastic box; this really did happen). This causes some amusement, especially when the attendees start thinking about paperclips as condoms. Before using asides like this you have to judge your audience, but it can all help to make a totally trivial prize into a major factor of interest.

Toys

We never entirely lose our childhood delights. This is a very practical fact that can be made use of in the training environment. We like toys. They can be of much greater value as prizes than their immediate value suggests. Part of the reason for this is in the obvious dichotomy between the way we feel we 'should' react to toys and the way we actually do. Because many of us try to hide our enjoyment of toys we are less likely to buy them for ourselves than other luxuries — so getting them as a prize gives an extra fillip.

At one extreme we could be dealing with actual toys. Go to any toy superstore and you will see rack on rack of pocket-money toys that make excellent prizes for training sessions. Look for something active or touchy-feely. Small games go down well too. There's an intermediate class of toy that covers computer games. Somehow these are more acceptable than most toys. It is also possible to target a computer game, for entertainment value (eg using a 'Tell Your Future with the Tarot' CD-ROM as a prize for a group of strategists) or genuine interest (eg golf games for older managers).

The easiest type of toy to choose is the executive toy, or other typical corporate giveaway. These typically have least impact in the session — part of the power of giving someone an inflatable alien is the reaction of the other trainees — but might be particularly appreciated. I still use a credit card travel alarm that I won at a conference, which is very much this type of toy.

Tools

It is possible to aim prizes in such a way that they have added learning leverage too. This is fine, as long as the prize doesn't appear too worthy or (frankly) dull. If you are going to take this approach, make sure there are some silly prizes too, so your whole approach doesn't seem too calculated. Appropriate books usually go down well, as does computer software that supports your training. Tools of the trade can be effective too — for instance, we've used stopwatches as prizes in facilitation training. If you aren't sure about the balance between practical tools and fun prizes, have a prize shelf with a row of different prizes and let the winners choose their own prize. Still have small silly spot prizes that are practically (and perhaps literally) thrown at the winner, but for occasional big prizes, give the winner a choice. Not only can they get what they like, but you get a chance to hone your choice of prizes, seeing what people go for... and don't.

Humour

Humour is an important factor in the prize-giving process. The aim is not to turn the training session into a competitive race where everyone is out to win at all costs. The prize is an incentive for contributing, or a way of feeding energy and interest back into a flagging group. Because of this, it's best if prizes are not awarded for conventional, quantitative skill-based performance. Instead the criteria should be qualitative (the idea I think is best) or near-random (whoever can come closest to a particular, unguessable answer). Keeping the prize sessions light and positive is often achieved by making them humorous. The prize activity should win the attention and enthusiasm of the trainees without irritating them when they don't win. Keeping it light and funny makes all the difference.

Giveaways

We can learn a lot from PR companies when it comes to the giveaway. If you send someone away from a course with only a pile of paper they are unlikely to look back on it with any great enthusiasm. Send them out with a smile on their face.

Chicago without the blues

In the build-up to launching Windows 95 in the UK, Microsoft organized a series of sessions for journalists called the Chicago Technology Tour. (This wasn't a flight over to the States – Chicago was the pre-launch code name of Windows 95.) The Microsoft PR agency, Text 100, made a brilliant use of giveaways, gradually building up the level with each session. At the first we got a Chicago Bulls fan pack with pennant and badge. At the second there was a tastefully embroidered Chicago Technology Tour rugby shirt. At the next there was a Chicago electronic game/alarm clock. At the final session, emphasizing the multimedia capabilities of Chicago, there was a pair of powered speakers for the PC, at the time a relative rarity. With maybe 50 journalists attending this cost a fair amount, but achieved a memorability that has rarely been equalled in such campaigns.

The giveaway is related to, but very different from, the prize (see above). It makes the same play on our delight in toys and gifts, but instead of being an incentive to contribute or an energizer, it is designed to reinforce the content after the event. When you see it, or use it, you are reminded of what was happening when you got it. For this reason, a good giveaway, like the Chicago sequence, should be something more likely to continue in use than a bumper sticker or a beer mat. Sometimes they can be practically relevant to the course (see page 000 on using books), but they don't have to be. One of my favourites, still in use, is a Swiss army knife. Look in any catalogue of promotional gifts, or the sort of 'amazing new technology gifts' catalogues that appear around Christmas, and you'll get a feel for the sort of thing that's possible.

The giveaway has two potential drawbacks – it can cost quite a lot of money, and it might seem wrong to bring an idea from the contaminated world of PR into the ethical world of training. The giveaway can certainly be misused. I once attended a series of conferences over several years for the managers of an in-house IT department. One of the big successes of the first conference was a toy duck in the bath of each delegate's room. Year after year, the organizers felt they had to go one better, until the goodie bag that delegates found in their room came to be quite extravagant. But by then it had lost impact. It was all too samey.

However, despite potential misuse this is still a powerful tool. PR is all about getting attention and retaining memory, both essential parts of the training and learning process. It would be silly to ignore the lessons that PR can bring to the training world. That's not to say that every PR gimmick is worth emulating. Take a specific example. A PC manufacturer, for reasons that escape me, included a pile of little black squares in a press release. When you opened the envelope they went all over the floor. It didn't go down well, irritating rather than entertaining. While such an item is memorable, it's the wrong sort of memories. Training reinforced with irritation is likely to induce a stubborn reaction, intentionally refusing to take the lesson.

In fact the PC manufacturer's gimmick proved to be a double backfire, as an irritated journalist started a rumour that some of the black squares were soaked in drugs, which didn't do the company's image any good, even though it was untrue.

Giveaways that have gone down well were things like the speakers and penknife I've already mentioned. Or an inflatable globe that my children enjoy. Or a well-designed shoulder bag with an exclusive design. Or a fascinating, pyramid-shaped clock. The key to effective giveaways seems to be that they should be useful, but a little different. They should amuse rather than irritate. They should have lasting value, so you keep using and keep referring to them. And they should be different – because when you've had 20 free pencils, the twenty-first lacks impact.

How about the cost issue? You shouldn't skimp on a giveaway. A nasty plastic diary or a pound shop present will insult and won't be kept around. (The only exception being if it's naff enough to be kitsch or such fun that you don't care it's cheap and nasty.) But this doesn't mean you have to blow your entire training budget. I'd recommend around the price of a commercial entertainment product – a CD or a video, say – for a typical giveaway resource. It's not a huge percentage of the cost of a day's training, and well worth it if it results in retention and a favourable impression of the trainers – a very desirable outcome if you are fighting for your existence like many in-house training regimes.

One final point that the CD reference made me think of. I wasn't specifically suggesting you give away a CD, just that it should provide an inflation-proof price reference. However, I was once presented with a CD as a giveaway, which almost got me into trouble. I'd still got the CD in my briefcase when I went into a music shop. As I came in, the alarm went off. On looking through my bag, it turned out that the CD still had the security tag on (luckily from a different shop). The shop kindly removed the tag for me, and I managed to put my foot in it even deeper by saying something like: 'I wouldn't mind, but I didn't even pay for it.' If you are using giveaways, make sure that the detail like this is handled properly.

Warm-ups

Training is an artificial situation. Short, sharp exercises, typically around five minutes in length, can be very valuable to break the ice with a new group, to increase energy levels and to get a group into a creative frame of mind. However, the warm-up has to be carefully pitched.

A senior manager speaks

'I can remember as if it were yesterday, the absolutely worst bit of training I ever undertook. There were many aspects of it that I found irritating. The trainers had obviously just been on a 'train the trainer' course on the subject. They knew nothing about management themselves. They had never managed anyone in their lives. Anything that deviated from the programmed format of the day was quite beyond them. And the catering was totally inappropriate.

'But the thing that immediately set things off on the wrong foot was the opening session. This was a management team-building day. I was with a group of seven other senior managers. We knew each other very well. We wanted to fine-tune the team, not bring an unknown group together. So what did they do? They started us with a childish party game where we had to recite everyone's name in a circle and say something about them. Even if I hadn't done this 10 times before at training sessions, it was pathetic with a group of people I already knew.'

There is a danger associated with the sort of reaction shown above. By their nature, warm-up exercises are inevitably close to silly games. The attendees need to be brought into the right frame of mind, and the warm-up session should have a clear objective even if it's not revealed until the end. As the exercise described above seems to be one with an objective of getting to know other people's names, it was totally inappropriate for an event where the attendees already knew each other. Such lack of preparation is inexcusable. Even if it wasn't known beforehand, the trainer should be able to pick this fact up from the attendees and switch the exercise.

Having a good resource pack of such exercises is an essential part of the trainer's repertoire. When putting together *Instant Teamwork* (see Appendix, page 184), a book of ice-breakers, warm-ups and timeouts, we looked at a wide range of the books aimed at providing games for trainers and found an awful lot of the material to be dull, unimaginative, lacking in fun and generally incapable of delivering the required result. Worthy is about the best adjective you can apply to it.

A good warm-up should incorporate energy and produce a change of direction — perhaps from listening to creative input, or in the case of ice-breakers, towards knowing the other course members better. Many of the techniques aimed at giving energy will involve movement — you can't get too much energy slumped in front of a table, dozing to the drone of a lecturer. If the intention is more to inspire greater creativity, the exercise might be more cerebral, but it still needs that boost of life. To give a feel for the sort of thing I mean, here are a couple of examples from *Instant Teamwork*. I've only included the exercise here — in the original there is more structure and detail. The first is a high-energy warm-up, the second an inspiration to think differently.

Fontastic

Each team is to produce a body font and capture it on digital camera or video. To do this, the team members spell out as many capital letters of the alphabet as they can, or a selected word, using only their bodies. One member of the team captures each letter using the camera (if using video, just a couple of seconds on each letter, not a video of the whole process). The role of camera operator must rotate every time to make sure everyone takes part.

The winning team is the one with the most legible letters — if there's a draw, decide on the quality of the font. This can be a riotously noisy activity, so make sure the environment is conducive to it. There's lots of energy and ice-breaking (difficult not to when you've been in such contortions together).

Ideas to get you fired

Split the group into teams, ideally three to five people each. Isolate the teams by using breakout rooms, or separating them as much as is possible in a single room. Each team spends five minutes brainstorming 'ideas to get you fired'. Encourage the teams to be wild and original. The teams should generate as many ideas as possible, each being a possible reason to lose your job. After generating ideas, the team should spend a minute choosing the idea they'd most like to put into action. Get the groups back together. Each team then has a minute to describe their favourite idea to the others. The other teams should come up with ways of making the idea practical.

When the teams come back together, forbid negative comment – only allow positive suggestions. This may involve modifying the idea, for example an idea involving killing someone (impractical) can be modified to finding a way to get them out of their job or into another job. This exercise is about enhancing creativity. By looking at anti-establishment ideas, the participants will break the constraints limiting their innovation. The result will be lots of impossible ideas, but even if they remain such, the participants will be in a freer frame of mind, and it is quite possible that an effective idea will be generated. This isn't the objective, but it may be an outcome.

Spur of the moment

A real problem with training is that trainers and the events themselves are often seen as rigid and inflexible. If you can respond effectively to a spur-of-the-moment remark you can often reduce this impression, and win over a potentially difficult trainee.

A sense of humour

I was attending a departmental training afternoon for managers. The form I was required to fill in before the event ended with a box labelled 'Any requests?' I could not resist writing 'anything by Van der Graaf Generator', a favourite band. When the event started and the organizer was going through the housekeeping, he pointed out this response to the other managers and presented me with a cassette of a Van der Graaf Generator album. This entirely unexpected sense of humour considerably changed my attitude to the organizer and the event.

The impact of this small gesture is much larger than it may at first seem. Several things are happening. As an individual, I'm surprised that someone has actually taken notice of something I said (or in this case, wrote). I might be slightly embarrassed to be singled out, but I really appreciate the fact that the organizer has gone out of his way to get me the tape. The rest of the attendees get a moment of light relief – it's an instant ice-breaker at the start of the session. And they too are impressed by the responsiveness.

A crucial contributor to getting it right when responding to a spur-of-the-moment remark is timing. The response has to be unexpected and as quick as possible. Take another example. I was giving a two-day creativity course at a major corporation. This was one of a series of courses that had been run for the new starters in a particular department. When my colleague asked what the attendees hoped to get out of the course, one of them said 'to play with some Play-Doh', referring to a previous year's exercise that he had heard about. We did not intend to use modelling clay this year, but the comment was noted.

A little later, we were trying out various creativity techniques with the course members working in small groups. One group decided to work on the problem of why a particular trainee could never get a date. Their (innovative but not yet made practical) solution was that he should get hold of a comedy puppet and use this to chat up prospective dates. The following morning, before we started the session, we presented the first attendee with some Play-Doh and the second with a glove puppet. The reaction was overwhelming, both from the individuals and from the group at large.

Of course the action has to be matched to the audience. This was a group of twenty-somethings, who found the whole thing hilarious. Having said that, surprisingly few groups won't respond if treated in the right way. The factor that impressed them most was the immediacy. They were used to training being something that was set in concrete. Here, at the earliest possible opportunity, there was a response. It was also almost certain that the giveaways came from the trainer's own pocket (they did), which enhanced the impact even more.

Spur of the moment doesn't have to be about a specific request. If you haven't got appropriate giveaways with you, it is sometimes possible to make a spur-of-the-moment response. In one example, a trainer was giving a session in a high street office. One of the attendees made a superb contribution. The trainer set them going on an exercise and ran out of the building, down the street to the nearest newsagent. She bought a bar of chocolate, ran back and presented it to the individual. Similarly, in a session I was giving in a building that housed a staff shop, I took the opportunity to use the coffee break to dash to the shop and buy some novelty items to give to members of a team who had just done particularly well in an exercise. In neither example was it necessary to make a point of having done this on the spur of the moment – it was obvious to those involved, and appreciated all the more because of it.

Most of all, a spur-of-the-moment gesture says that the trainer is human, and actually cares about the people he or she is training. This isn't a cold, calculated part of a programmed exercise, it is a human reaction to another human being. The examples above have mostly involved giving something, but the nature of the spur-of-the-moment action has to fit the stimulus. It may be as little as throwing in an extra war story to fit a trainee's query, or bringing forward part of the course in response to a particular interest of the group.

Because of the essential lack of calculation, it is important that spur-of-the-moment gestures don't become the expected norm. You should not go into a session thinking 'I've got three spur-of-the-moment actions to take between now and lunchtime.' You might go through half a dozen sessions without anything being required. The whole point is the spontaneity. What you do need in advance is the ability to see the opportunity for a spur-of-the-moment action and to have the will to carry that action through. It will usually involve you in putting yourself out in some way. But the effort will be more than outweighed by the result.

Software

Just as the books topic earlier in this section was not about using books as a means of training, but rather to extend the training after the event, so this is not about computer-based training. Software can be used very effectively as a resource to reinforce the message of the course.

From a follow-up feedback form:

> **The thing I've found most useful is the CD ROM, not for the course notes, which I haven't looked at, but the practical software has really helped me use what I learnt in a work context.**

This quote is not from a course on using software, but from one on creativity. It's not always the most obvious applications of software that generate the most benefits. With our creativity courses we give away a CD-ROM with a range of different resources to help the trainees to take their learning back into the workplace. These include:

● an HTML (Web-based) guide to finding out more about creativity with links to online creativity sites and information about creativity books;
● software to help map and structure thoughts and ideas;
● software to evaluate alternatives;
● software to stimulate the generation of new ideas and solving problems.

The software takes the course as a starting point and enables any attendees who wish to go further to get deeper into the subject. At the same time, the practical tools help the trainees to make use of what they have learnt and to reinforce the message in the crucial first months.

Producing a CD-ROM is neither technically complex nor expensive any more. The ease with which HTML can be developed using an off-the-shelf package like Microsoft FrontPage or Adobe PageMill means that it is not a highly technical task to construct a Web-style front end to the CD which can both put across information that extends the course and introduce any software provided on the CD.

The great advantage of using an HTML approach (apart from the ease of building an interactive hypertext document this way) is that it is possible to make transparent links into the World Wide Web. The same browser that will be used to explore the CD will be the mechanism for getting out to the Web. As long as the trainee has Web access from the computer on which the CD is used, it will be possible to click on a link from your CD and move out anywhere on the Web. This way, you not only have your own resources to extend the learning, but also can point trainees at this vast library of possibilities.

Using software this way fits fairly comfortably with a traditional training approach, even if the means of executing it and the degree of extensibility go far beyond anything that was possible before. However, it is possible to go still further. Take the creativity example above. Not only is there an information section on the CD, but a collection of software supporting three crucial aspects of creativity: generating ideas and solving problems, structuring ideas and discussions, and evaluating different options. One of the pieces of software supplied was specifically written to support and follow the course. The others are (legally copied) off-the-shelf products.

If it is possible to get a piece of bespoke software professionally and cheaply written to support your course, it can be a very cost-effective way of making sure that the benefits of the training are reaped. The idea here is not just to repeat the message of the course, but to provide a tool to put what has been learnt into practice. It might be as simple as a macro for a word processor or spreadsheet. In the creativity example, we use a fairly sophisticated piece of software written in Visual Basic that contains many of the techniques covered in our training, the framework that links them together and the opportunity to input your own requirements and work through the techniques to come up with ideas. This sort of product, which took a couple of months' work for an experienced programmer to develop, might seem too expensive to put together, but it is often the case that in-house programming teams have opportunities to develop such packages either as a training project or as a spare-time development.

Distributing third-party software products sounds equally expensive; however, there are a number of ways of managing the cost here. If there is a reasonably priced product that matches your requirement (this may need some searching around – the Web is a good source), you may well be able to negotiate a licence to reproduce the software at significantly less than the list price with a bulk order. Even more cost-effectively, you can use shareware. This is software that can be freely distributed. Usually there will be some limitations on the software – for example it might expire after a month's use, or have some facilities like printing or saving disabled.

The advantage of using shareware in this way is that you can provide a wide range of packages to help your trainees put their training experience to practical use. The trainees can try out the different packages without cost. If at that stage they decide that a package will help them, it is up to them (or their company) to pay for the software – it doesn't come off the training budget. But despite being cheap and cheerful, the software has reinforced the message and will provide long-term support if the trainee decides to purchase it. There is a wide range of very professional shareware available now. It is not a route that many large companies have taken in the past, but for this type of training resource it can prove invaluable. There is a section in the Appendix on finding appropriate products.

Quick tip

If you put HTML onto a CD ROM for use in training, it is possible to set up the CD so that it will automatically open a page when it is put into the PC. By including a file called autorun.inf in the main directory of the CD ROM, you can start a program automatically. This file is a simple text file, which should contain the following text:

```
[autorun]
open = myprog.exe
```

… where *myprog* is the name of the program you want to run. Unfortunately the autorun format is not clever enough for you to be able to specify the name of an HTML file and have it automatically pop up on the screen. For the purposes of kicking off an HTML page, you need a small program that will load a Web page into a browser. If you need one of these, drop me an e-mail at brian@cul.co.uk and I will be happy to e-mail one to you free of charge.

4E DEVELOPMENT

Training does not happen spontaneously. Course development is a major part of the lifecycle of any successful training organization. Once courses have been produced they should not be static entities. There is some similarity with the prototyping of a physical product. A first run of a training course will produce plenty of opportunities to feed back changes and make new developments. Making good use of feedback is an essential component of development.

It's true that all good events these days elicit comments from trainees, but there are two problems that degrade the value of this feedback. It is boring for the trainees to fill in the forms, and all too often nothing is seen to be done as a result of the painstaking collection and assessment of responses – it's as if the action of taking feedback was a talisman that achieved success in its own right. These topics look at making feedback more interesting for the trainees, and making training flexible enough to be able to respond to feedback from session to session.

In the process of developing new courses, we now have an unrivalled resource in the Internet. Those developing courses should be using the Internet as a matter of course – we also consider the best approach to mine this rich seam of content and materials. We begin, though, with creativity. If your training is not to be a clone of someone else's work, there has to be some creativity in the production and development of the training. Fostering such creativity should be a prime concern.

Key topic – Creativity techniques

Creativity plays a key role in the development of new forms of training, and of making training more accessible. The appetite for new approaches is immense – training needs to continue evolving, keeping trainees satisfied as they become more and more sophisticated.

Behind it

This technique, taken from *Instant Creativity* (see Appendix, page 180), is a great way of developing new methods and approaches.

At the heart of every problem is a need. Very often this need occurs in many other circumstances. This technique expands thinking by looking at other areas where this need might occur.

The first thing to do is to identify the essential need in your problem, or at least one of the fundamentals. For instance, if you are trying to design seating, your essential need might be comfort, it might be style, or even fireproofing. Next think of three examples of this need in a different area. Taking style, we could think of clothes design, car design and the club scene as examples where style is important.

Finally, relate the external areas back to the problem. How can we apply clothes design to seating? An easy answer is to put whatever is happening on the catwalks onto our seats. From car design we could focus on the centre of gravity – putting the driver at the heart of the seat. We could focus on streamlining. We could even take an inapplicable area of car design like fuel efficiency and ask how this could be applied. (An efficient build process for the seating would minimize effort in sitting and rising, or building a table into the seat would make human fuel intake easier.)

You could try combining needs. Given the seating example above we could combine fashion design with old slippers (comfort) and try to find an area of stimulation in this. This is tougher to do and you might want to become experienced with the technique before doing so.

Creativity is a strange topic. Schools spend years suppressing the natural creativity of students, emphasizing that there is only one right answer – the one that the teacher has in mind. Survival also teaches that creativity is dangerous. Any caveman who took a creative approach and pulled faces at a wild animal rather than running away did not have time to write up his experiment. Yet relying entirely on experience is just as risky. The result is tunnel vision, ignoring the fact that the world is changing at an immense pace. Business needs creativity or it dies. As Tom Peters puts it, 'creativity and zest have become the prime creators of economic value'. In the training world, creativity comes in everywhere – but one prime example is in the development of new courses.

It's a common assumption that creativity is something you have or haven't got, yet appropriate techniques can bring out anyone's creative potential. Since the 1950s, creativity experts have been devising techniques for stimulating creativity to the extent that it is now a practical business discipline. Traditional management practices pre-date the current frenetic pace of change; creativity is one of a new set of skills necessary to manage in today's business environment.

Creativity is like an under-used muscle: it needs exercise to build it up. Try this: spend a minute devising a way to use a single spoon to feed one hundred people simultaneously. Don't cheat – do the exercise first, then read on. A single minute is all I ask.

There are many ways to use a single spoon to feed a hundred people. It could be a solid gold spoon, which you sell, taking them for a meal with the proceeds. It could be a huge edible spoon made out of pizza. It could be a restaurant in the shape of a spoon. And so on. Think this is cheating? Yes, but it's practical cheating. These are legitimate solutions, making different assumptions about the spoon.

This example isn't a fully fledged creativity technique. Normally such techniques remove self-imposed barriers, then return to normality to provide a realistic outcome. Nevertheless, the spoon is a handy reminder of how easy it is to try to solve a problem with incomplete information. I never said that the spoon was of a conventional size and made of stainless steel.

In training terms we are constantly imposing assumptions about what, how and where training should take place. At the same time we are facing tighter budgets and the need to come up with more effective, more attractive training courses and methods. There has never been more need for creativity, and the application of systematic creativity is a much more reliable approach than sitting back and waiting for inspiration or using the overused technique of brainstorming.

This isn't the place to develop your creativity skills in depth, though do try out the technique detailed in the mini-case. To find out more about the potential for using creativity techniques, see the books in the creativity section in the appendix (page 179), and check out the free software for creativity support, book references and much more at the Creativity Unleashed Web site www.cul.co.uk.

Most of all, bear in mind that creativity isn't a nice option to polish up the detail of your training – it's an essential at the core of what you do. With it, your training can be flexible, powerful and cost-effective. Without it, the best you can hope for is me-too training, copying the best that others achieve without enhancing it. Without it, there is no *Training+*. As such, it should be a subject that demands significant attention.

Finding your materials

The Web isn't just a resource for your trainees; it can also provide an excellent source for information and materials in the development of your training. All you need to be able to do is to find your way around.

Getting the goods

For a recent presentation I needed images as widely separated as a picture of David and Goliath and a diagram of the workings of a CD drive. All were found on the Web in seconds.

It's worth remembering that copyright may apply to items on the Web just as much as it may do to a printed page (it doesn't matter whether or not a copyright symbol is displayed). That 'may' is an absolute minefield, which is going to make a lot of lawyers happy (and rich) bunnies for many years. After all, if someone in China, connecting to the Web through a Russian-owned ISP, downloads a picture from my UK-owned Web site, which is hosted on servers sited in the USA but owned by another UK company, whose copyright laws come into play?

Often there isn't a problem. It is highly unlikely that anyone is going to complain about downloading anything you find on the Web to your PC for private use (in fact, as UK legislators discovered in 1999, this is almost impossible to avoid thanks to the caching technique used by Web browsers). Many Web-site owners will be happy about you using extracts from their sites in closed training sessions and presentations, provided you give appropriate recognition of the source. But electronic documents and pictures are too easy to copy and pirate. Unless the Web site explicitly describes the content as freely copyable, check with the site's owners before reproducing anything.

In the past few years the Internet has provided a huge new resource for training developers. Sadly, many of them have chosen to make little use of it. It's as if the world's biggest library and communications centre had been dumped on your desktop, only to be ignored. This is to some extent understandable, because the Internet's speed of growth has been unparalleled in history. As recently as 1996 it could sensibly have been described as worthless to business – now it is an essential.

Many of those who reject the Internet as an effective resource dislike the word 'library' in this context. They argue that the Internet, and specifically the World Wide Web, isn't a library. That's not true. As I point out in the quote on page 36, it is, in effect, just a vast library that has huge open windows through which anyone can throw anything from a single page to a whole encyclopaedia. This strange nature means that it has disadvantages. The contents are not verified. There is no structure. There might be vast amounts of information on a trivial topic and nothing at all on something very important. But on the other hand, you don't have to keep quiet, you can skip from reference to reference in seconds, there's no censorship, there's interactivity and there's excitement. And you don't have to go out in the rain to get to it.

The positive aspects of the Internet make it an ideal resource for anything from images to theory and exercises – as long as you can find the content that you want. The near-anarchy that is one of the Internet's great strengths also makes it difficult to navigate. Of course there are search engines, but they are not the universal panacea that some suggest. Each has limitations and advantages – to make the most of the Internet you need to know more about the tools that are available to get to the information you want. Consider a quick four-point plan:

1. Explore search engines and catalogues. You may have your favourite, but each gives different results. Word-level engines like AltaVista are better when you are looking for specific keywords. Structured catalogues like Yahoo! are better when you know what you are looking for, but not what it's called (though the distinction between search engines and catalogues is becoming blurred). UK-based engines will often yield very different results to the more familiar US products. And each engine has special syntax for homing in on a specific requirement. You might not know each in detail, but it's worth investigating the workings of your favourites. See the Appendix (page 182) for more on search engines.
2. Consider using multiple search engines simultaneously. You can do this with a meta-search engine on the Web or you can run software on your PC that accesses various engines and pulls back the results. While this approach can't use the more subtle forms of search query,

it can pull in a wider span of results – ideal if you aren't getting anywhere.

3. Use topic-specific sources, like the excellent Training Zone (see page 185 for more information).

4. Remember that the Internet is more than the Web. Consider the network of people whose e-mail addresses you know – could one of them help you with your requirement? And check out the powerful resources available from newsgroups, provided you observe appropriate etiquette.

Taking on these four points isn't going to make you a Web guru, but it will help improve your use of the Web. To really get the benefits that the Internet will bring, see *Mining the Internet* in the Appendix (page 183).

Flexible development

Modern technology makes it possible to dispose of the dilemma that often faces training developers. You want your training to be professional – hence using materials with a long preparation lead time – but you also want to be flexible enough to respond to changing requirements and feedback from trainees.

Digging a pit

In a regular creativity training seminar I was giving, I found that each time I gave the session I was apologizing for one line on one slide. It had seemed a great idea when I devised the course, but somehow, each time I brought it up I found I was having to explain what it was all about and got into an unnecessary tangle that left the trainees baffled. It was a diversion from the point that I found enjoyable, but it simply didn't work. Because of taking a flexible development approach, I could drop the line from the slide in subsequent sessions, learning from practical experience. Such fine-tuning can make all the difference between a good course and a brilliant one.

The case study in *Surprise packages* (page 111) involved rewriting a session based on feedback from the attendees. This was part of a series of repeated seminars which had to be highly professional and have the polish of an expensive course. Traditionally this would have been a real problem. The slides (35 mm or overhead) and the handouts would be professionally printed with a high overhead and long turn-round. The session itself would probably be formalized word-for-word. Unfortunately, while such a fixed approach might have looked professional, it would have crippled our ability to respond to feedback and changing circumstances.

New technology – particularly using computer projection for visual aids, and producing handouts in-house – means that it is now possible to make changes to a session each time it is given. This can be immensely valuable, not just at the detailed level that was shown in the *Surprise packages* example. Changes could be simple corrections of errors, introduction of the latest data, or taking out a single slide or line that hasn't gone well as in my example above.

Flexibility of this sort is only relevant to a training session that is given more than once, but under such circumstances it is possible to take a prototyping approach to development. The first time the session is run, the trainer should work through what went well and what went badly. If there is any possibility of having a colleague sit in on the session and provide an objective view, so much the better. There is also the opportunity to take guidance from the feedback given by the trainees.

Given this information, the course designer can look at how to make the aspects that went well even better and to correct any problem areas. After the first session it may be necessary to make major changes to the course design. Subsequently it is more likely to be fine-tuning that is incorporated. This approach seems obvious, yet it is surprising how infrequently it is taken. A flexibly designed course evolves with time, selecting the parts of the course that are fittest and bringing in new components, in good Darwinian fashion.

There is an inevitable concern about being over-driven by feedback, and hence thrashing about with the course to try to follow the whims of individual groups of people. This would only the case if your flexible development was... inflexible. It shouldn't be the case that as soon as you get a piece of feedback you inevitably modify the course to match it. However, if the feedback strikes a chord – if you find yourself thinking, 'yes, that makes sense' – or if you find the same feedback coming up in several sessions, the flexible approach gives you the opportunity to do something about it.

Moving to flexible development does require a different attitude to preparation for courses. There has to be more of a 'just in time' preparation of materials. It is not sensible, for instance, to produce all the handouts for a series of sessions up front. There will be costs attached to this approach, and it will require more flexibility from the course designer, but the outcome is well worth the effort.

Some resources remain inviolate. If, for example, you are giving away a book as part of your course, you can't change that every time you tweak the contents of the course. But this does not invalidate the principle. The fixed elements are liable to be waypoints in the course, rather than making up the whole of the content. It's easy enough, in fact it's advantageous, to be able to make changes while maintaining those fixed points for reference.

Ideas – stealing and creating

The key topic of this section was about being creative. When you are developing new training, creativity is essential. But there is another great source too – stealing ideas.

Immature poets imitate; mature poets steal.

T.S. Eliot, The Sacred Wood

Eliot had it just right. Copying what others are doing is a starting point, but it's not the way to greatness. Instead you need to steal elements of what others do and merge it with your own originality. Don't take this as any criticism of the creative process. You need to be generating plenty of new ideas, and the creativity techniques described in the key topic on page 140 are the best way to get them. But to work in isolation from the rest of the world would be to ignore a huge fund of possibilities. (An entertaining aside – very similar quotes are also ascribed to Picasso and Stravinsky. Who was stealing from whom?)

Looking elsewhere

A major factor in picking up ideas that will really seem new, rather than copying other trainers, is to look outside the field of training. The world is full of great ideas, almost all of them not produced by trainers. Sorry if this hurts. I know we're incredibly intelligent, idea-rich people, but so is everyone else, and we're outnumbered. As well as looking at what other trainers are doing, studying other courses and online learning modules, start looking at the rest of the world.

There are two ways of going about your day-to-day business. You can be ruthlessly focused on the task in hand, or you can take in everything that is around you. I've nothing against focus. When you are engaged in an activity, whatever it is, giving it your whole focus is the only way to guarantee to give the 100 per cent delivery that will differentiate you from all the rest. But there are plenty of in-between times, such as when you are travelling, or just slumped in front of the TV at home. There are good reasons for abandoning focus at this point. In fact, you owe it to yourself to do so. Unless you can switch off, you will be imposing unwanted stress on yourself. If you sit at home watching TV, or walk down the street, constantly picking at the latest work problem, you are not doing yourself any favours. Instead, consciously disengage from your work focus. Don't plan or rehearse. Just take in what is around you. Observe. Let your observations be your focus.

If this sounds dangerously close to Zen and the Art of Training, don't worry. There's a very practical reason – because as you take in what you see and hear you will come across items that interest you. It could be something as simple as the way the conductor on the train works down the carriage. It could be a piece of information. Make a note. Because often the inspiration to do something different with your training (or anything else, for that matter) will come from well outside your field of interest.

You might get an idea about putting a point across from advertising. You might pick up a tip on feedback in a restaurant. Your bank statement could give you some ideas on planning personal training. The important thing is to remain open. Don't close down and criticize your own ideas before they are fully formed. New ideas are like green shoots – all too easy to trample on. When you see something that interests you, even if you can't think of an application immediately, capture it for future possible use.

Picking up a book

You don't have to sit around and wait for the external lesson that you need to appear so you can trip over it. You can get out there and look for it. Where better to find inspiration than in a book? But not a book on training. How wide is your reading? Do you stick to training books? It is time to break open your reading habits. Not just a little bit, but smashing them open to take in a much wider range of books.

I find business biographies are a great source of ideas – those books that explore both the workings of a business and the people behind it. Usually there is something special about the company – or there wouldn't be a book – and that special something can be very stimulating. Equally, though, ideas can come from fiction, from popular science, from the whole gamut of the library. Reading as many different books as you can with an open mind will provide a treasury of ideas to steal from.

To get you started, there is a small exposure-widening section in the Appendix (see page 183). But don't limit yourself to this. Be a frequent visitor to bookshops. Browse the online shops. Get more books into your life, and make sure that you surprise yourself at regular intervals.

From magazine, via TV, to Web

Books seem ideally placed to provide that invitation to steal because the printed word forces you to use your imagination as you read. But there are plenty of other media opportunities to inspire you. Again, the secret is a catholic interest in the widest possible range of sources. Don't just read the training magazines, trawl widely varying subjects looking for inspiration. Keep your eye open when watching TV. And don't forget the Web.

We've already seen (page 143) how the Internet can be a source of materials. Also be prepared to scan more broadly for ideas to steal. Take half an hour on a regular basis to skip from site to site, following links on a whim. Look at how the Web site itself presents the information. Look at the content. Be open to the ideas you can lift.

That's a nice idea...

Most of this topic is on looking outside your own sphere, because that's where there is most new opportunity. There are many more external sources than there are pure training sources, and their ideas will be foreign, novel and exciting when brought into the training context. This doesn't mean, though, that you should ignore the opposition. Other trainers and training companies will have ideas that are worth taking on board.

Bear in mind the distinction between ideas and material. Text and images are copyright, but ideas and concepts aren't. This isn't an invitation to lift chunks of text from a competitor's course, but you can certainly learn a lot about how to do things better, and what you aren't doing at all. If your budget is reasonably large, you ought to be regularly sending your trainers on other companies' courses to keep up with the competition. If cash is very tight, look out for reviews and write-ups. Get brochures for courses – they're free. However you approach it, condense out the key ideas that make the course and the approach different. Then go about stealing the idea and building on it with the unique content of your experience.

Fun feedback

Feedback is boring. It is a low-reward activity for the trainees. So what do we do? Finish a course with it? That's like going out of your way to end your training with a whimper rather than a bang. There has to be a better way.

Paper planes

For a range of reasons, the afternoon session of a course had been particularly dull. The trainer (not entirely to blame) had only the feedback session left before he sent out his trainees, feeling pretty down about the whole experience. He thought quickly, then produced a pile of blank sheets of paper. He placed a large cardboard box at the front of the training room, with a table some distance away. Then he addressed the trainees.

'We've had a good day today, but I'd like to make sure things are even better in the future, so I want to get a bit of feedback from you.' (Groans) 'But the good news is that there is no form to fill in. I've put a pile of paper here. Take as many sheets as you like. On each sheet write your name and one comment. It has to be constructive – either highlighting a good feature of the course, or suggesting a way of improving part of it. Then I'd like you to make it into a paper plane and throw it into the box. Stand behind the table to do that. Every comment will be read, whether or not it makes the box, but we'll be sending out prizes next week for each real suggestion that makes it into the box. The more of your suggestions get in there, the better the prize.'

The trainer had more feedback than ever before, and the trainees left visibly uplifted. The usually depressing feedback process had actually recovered the session and sent them out on a high.

There is no denying the value of good feedback to the trainer (at least as long as it is used effectively – see *Flexible development* above), but it's a thankless task for trainees. This in itself reduces the value of feedback, because there is limited incentive for the trainee to put any effort into making the feedback useful.

Making feedback fun should address both the mechanism for giving it and the process of recording and collecting it. In the case study above, the key elements were a fun collection process and a reward for volume of constructive ideas. These are only two of the contributory factors.

Timing and location

It's natural enough to think that feedback has to be given at the end of the session and in the training room. After all, it's difficult to give feedback before you've had the experience that you are commenting on, and it's hard to resist the urge to make use of the captive audience. Yet, as we have seen, this is often not a good point to get cooperation from a group of people who are probably most interested in getting home.

There are a number of opportunities to come at these aspects of feedback more creatively. Try, for instance, getting feedback before the session starts. Ask people what they think their response is going to be. Then, at the end, just ask them what's different and why. You can, of course, collect feedback as you go, through the day. This is more effective in that the participants can remember better how they felt about a specific part of the course, but it loses an overview of the whole and can get tedious.

Alternatively, make feedback the penultimate session of the day, leaving the final slot to something light and uplifting that won't require any feedback. That way, you don't send people out feeling depressed.

When it comes to location, the main concern is actually getting the feedback at all. The sad fact (which shows just what your trainees think of giving feedback, valuable feedback in itself) is that if you send them out with a feedback form to fill in off site, they are much less likely to use it. Look for alternatives to boost the response. Try giving feedback forms to take away in the lunch session or at breaks. If you are going to send them away with a form, make sure there's an incentive to send it back (over and above being helpful). Or totally separate the feedback from the event, making use of e-mail to bring the feedback request to the trainee's desktop.

Idea generation

It is important in getting feedback to ask 'how well did we do?', but only to do this is to miss a huge opportunity. You have a captive audience who are in your target market and who can be asked 'what can we do to make it better?' When you do this, you are asking your trainees to indulge in idea generation. All too often we expect the trainees to sit down and come up with ideas off the top of their head, usually with the time pressure that they can leave as soon as they've finished – so it should be no surprise that there are rarely any great ideas coming out of this process. It has to be managed like any other idea-generation session.

The most popular answer to this challenge would be to hold a brainstorming session. Unfortunately, although brainstorming is the most commonly used approach to idea generation, it is stunningly inappropriate. To go straight into a brainstorm shows a sad lack of understanding of creativity. In effect there are two sorts of creativity – the generation of new ideas is quite separate from the development and combination of ideas. The original generation process is an individual activity. Individual people come up with ideas (hence the comments about a camel being a horse designed by a committee). Putting people into a group actually suppresses idea generation. What the group is good for is taking those ideas, combining and refining them – and that's where the brainstorm comes in.

In fact the inventor of brainstorming, Alex Osborn, never intended it to be used in isolation. He always expected a creativity technique to be used to generate ideas first, then the brainstorm to bring them together and modify them. To use brainstorming alone is a bit like trying to use a fountain pen without ink. You can scratch a letter, but it's nowhere near as effective as it could be. The ideal approach, then, is to give your trainees a few minutes alone, using a creativity technique individually, then bring them together for a five-minute brainstorm. Some ideas of creativity techniques are in the section *Creativity techniques* (page 140) – otherwise see the Appendix for further reading.

Recording and collection

The traditional mechanism for the recording and collection of feedback is a form, handed in at the end of the session. We have already seen the opportunity to use paper planes or e-mail. Consider other alternatives.

For broad-brush feedback, you could use the method used by the House of Commons. Have two doors to pass through, one for each message. Feedback then becomes as simple as the way you leave. Or have a range of rubbish bins with different weightings to throw your post-session scrap paper in.

Just moving away from a traditional form to fill in can help. Consider covering a wall with paper and have trainees spray their feedback as graffiti. Or give them picture postcards to send with the feedback on. If you use response scales (something like 1 for a disaster to 10 for a great session), give them something physical to manipulate (anything from an abacus to a piece of modelling clay) to reflect the scale, or use arty computer graphics. This is a great area for the *Using what's around* technique (see page 33). Look at the materials available to you and see how they can be used creatively in recording or collecting feedback. Anything might suggest an option. For instance, perhaps you've got lots of junk CDs lying around. Give each trainee a CD for each of the criteria you want scored (write the criterion on the CD using an indelible marker, or use a stick-on CD label). Then make a simple scoring rack with a peg for each score that fits through the hole in the CD. It's simple but much more fun than a filling in a form.

Rewards

Never forget the power of reward if you want to get something done. At the most basic level, you could enter all the returned forms into a draw for a prize – or give a small prize to each returnee. As we saw in the case study, this can be extended to give a better prize if there are more impressive results. You can make these prizes instant by giving away lottery scratch cards in exchange for a set of feedback, or by having a lucky dip of goodies on the way out of the session. Rewards don't have to be big and flashy – just some encouragement that means there's an answer to 'what's in it for me?' With a reward, everyone benefits from the feedback.

Evaluating benefits

The evaluation of the benefits of training — or more properly, a cost/benefit analysis — is an essential part of training development. Benefits should be predicted before the event and assessed in hindsight. However, such an exercise should be seen as a learning vehicle, not a way of ascribing blame.

Real-world views

The chief internal auditor of a large company was assessing the costs and benefits of a course for his department. When he had totalled up the costs, they far outweighed the benefits in financial terms. The course was cancelled. Yet the few attendees who had managed to go on the course were giving vastly improved customer service. When a little while later a number of staff members were promoted, a high percentage were from the group who had attended the course. Something strange was happening.

Cost/benefit analysis is frequently painful because costs are much easier to assess than benefits. Costs tend to be solidly financial, and (relatively) easy to pin down. Benefits, on the other hand, are much more hypothetical before the event, and often have components that aren't immediately financial. For instance, take a case where training three customers results in them staying with your company when otherwise they would have gone to a competitor. If each spends £1 million a year with your company, it is arguable that the benefits of the course include that £3 million — but it is very hard to prove it.

This difficulty does not mean that benefits should not be evaluated, but that care should be taken not to overvalue costs in the equation, and to make sure that the total impact of the training is taken into account. Where the outcome of the exercise is negative, showing that the costs actually outweighed the benefit, this should be seen as a learning tool, not the trigger for a hunt for a scapegoat to take responsibility for the loss. After all, projected figures are by definition guesswork — attempts to explain every penny of difference from reality are futile excursions into fantasy.

When assessing the benefits, look at all the potential stakeholders. Each is liable to have their own, distinct benefits. For example:

Trainees

- improved performance;
- more job satisfaction;
- more transferable skills;
- less pressure on those with the skills;
- more flexibility.

Managers

- able to use workforce more flexibly;
- able to cover requirement;
- more efficient staff;
- fewer employee relations problems;
- better products and services.

Customers

- improved service;
- better opinion of company.

... and so on. The art of assessing benefits is to look into each area of impact of training and to discover (as much as is possible) exactly how the training will impact upon the stakeholders (and subsequently has). This can be monitored to some extent after the event with satisfaction questionnaires, but a lot of the benefit impact assessment has to come from those who are close to the stakeholder – for example, the customer service staff as well as the customers themselves.

Some of the benefits will not have direct financial implications. You might genuinely want a happier workforce and be prepared to put some money into it, even if there isn't an obvious financial benefit. In practice, a happier workforce tends to be more productive and efficient, but even without this benefit it's an aim that might be given some value. Equally, when assessing financial impact, beware of the 'if we only' argument. An example of this would be to say that the stakeholder customers spend

£20 million a year with the company. The argument then goes 'if we only make a 1 per cent improvement in customer spend, that's £200,000. The training is bound to have at least this impact, so it's worth doing'. Big numbers make this sort of non-logic quite attractive. The aim should be to find benefits with a clearer link to the training than this.

It is most important when looking at benefit that we don't use the measures that are easy to monitor, rather than the measures that are important. If necessary be prepared to have benefit statements that temporarily have blank boxes, rather than fill in the numbers you have, however irrelevant they might be. And once again, don't confuse forecasts and projections with reality. All too often you are encouraged only to ask 'how well did the training do against the objectives?' This is useful, especially when setting the next set of objectives, but it shouldn't be the sole measure. The actual benefit to the company is much more important than the match to objectives that were, inevitably, only a guess at what would be needed in the future.

4F TARGETING AND MARKETING

Before any training takes place there has to be an assessment of need, and arrangements made for the training to take place. All too often these assessments are isolated, while invitations to attend training are too much driven by company policy rather than individual needs – yet every trainer will acknowledge the huge difference between the person who actively wants to learn and the person who is a prisoner on a course.

At the same time, we have recognized that training is always under threat when cash or time is short, so part of this section, which is very much about taking a business viewpoint on training, is making sure that the need for training (and for the people who give the training) is clearly identified. From there we can move on to getting the trainees onto the courses. Whether this is an in-house seminar or a commercial event, this can be a non-trivial task.

It may seem Machiavellian to put topics about the politics of survival and running training as a business in with these apparently more practical topics, but realistically political subjects are just as essential to making sure that effective training happens. We can't afford to sweep them under the carpet, as has happened so often in the past.

The topics in this section look at new ways to manage these crucial, business-oriented aspects of the process.

Key topic – Matching the individual

There is nothing new in the requirement to match the training to the individual, whether through personal development plans or other approaches. Yet there has been a mismatch between the theory and the reality. It's time for a new look at developmental matchmaking.

Square pegs and round holes

June was a secretary. She was a very good secretary – highly regarded by her boss and everyone who dealt with her. When it came to her career review, her boss suggested she go on the PA Academy, a training scheme set up by the company to provide secretaries with the skills needed to make them into the next generation of personal assistant. June seemed strangely reluctant.

Two weeks later, June's boss had a call from another manager. She had applied for a job as a PC support agent. The natural assumption that a very good secretary would want to fulfil the super-secretarial role of PA was false. No one had asked June what she wanted. If she had been forced into the PA Academy, the result would have been a total waste of the training budget. Instead, she took IT training and moved into the support department, where she is now a supervisor.

There's an uncomfortably philosophical bit of thinking required at the heart of this topic. It's all very well to talk about having a plan to develop an individual, but there's a danger of taking an oversimplistic view. A sculptor sometimes says that a piece of wood or a piece of stone had the particular sculpture in it, waiting to be revealed by the artist. The personal development plan takes something of a similar approach to a human being. But unfortunately (for the plan, that is, but fortunately for us) people are much more complex than a piece of wood.

Before you can sensibly say how a person should be developed you need to have a picture of where they are going – and that picture can only really come from them. I use variants on the following technique shamelessly in many of my books because it is so valuable, and it should be the starting point for matching the training to the individual. The 'you' in this case is the potential trainee.

Take a sheet of paper and divide it into two. In the left-hand column jot down the main activities you undertake – between 10 and 20. Don't differentiate between work and social activities – list everything significant. Also extend back along the timeline. What did you do years ago that you were good at, but haven't done since? Similarly, think yourself into the future. Is there anything that you've never actually done, but think you would be good at? This is not a matter of impossible dreams, but talents you feel you may well have, given the chance.

Now the fun bit. Imagine you have come into a huge sum of money. You will never have to work again. Take a minute to enjoy the thought and its immediate implications. On the other half of the paper, draw up two columns: 'Yes' and 'No'. Assign all your activities to one or other of the columns. What would you do anyway? What would you instantly dismiss?

Now add to the list any major personal goals that you might have – anything from short to very long term. Phrase them as activities to keep them consistent. For example, a goal of becoming a manager would make the activity 'managing a team of people'. Make sure these are all still 'Yes' items if you were very rich. Now run through the list with a second piece of paper alongside. Jot down any skills you would have to gain to make the 'Yes' items happen. Where there's an activity you already do well (don't be modest, be honest), how could you be even better, to make it an area of expertise? If there's an activity you don't do well, what would you need to change? Is it realistically possible? – if so, outline very briefly a programme that would achieve the change.

The outcome of this exercise is a personal development plan driven not by organizational need (see *Wants vs Needs* below for more on the organizational requirement) but by personal goals. This is extremely important. All too often business processes fail to recognize the huge importance of personal goals. 'What's in it for me' sounds selfish and unprofessional, but it is the underlying driver of most business relationships, and it is much better if it's out in plain sight. By ensuring that the primary driver of training is the individual, there is a much better chance of getting the training done and of having it made use of.

The second stage of matching is prioritization. We now have an unstructured list of potential developments, some long term, some short term. The aim should be to highlight the 20 per cent of developments that are likely to carry 80 per cent of the benefit (in good Pareto fashion). Perform the rating exercise twice, once from the individual's viewpoint, once from the organization's. Given that all these developments fit in with the individual's goals, it is reasonable that some of the selection should be based on organizational priorities.

Finally, make the selection. Aim to choose a collection of areas for action in a particular year. You should include some from each of the personal and organizational priorities. Make sure also that there is a mix of short-term and long-term requirements. The result should be a well-balanced spell of training. Making a plan for a year makes sense, but bear in mind that external factors could change priorities in a shorter timescale, and be prepared to make changes flexibly.

There is one concern some have with this trainee-centred approach. In the case study on page 162, I, as manager, had a very clear picture of what the trainees who worked for me needed. Although some of them would have very strongly identified the need for better people skills, others would have shied away from the area, or have not regarded it as interesting enough. It is often the case that an individual will need help in identifying the obstacles that are getting in the way of personal goals, a role that a manager may have to fulfil, but this does not invalidate the individual as the core driver. It was still the individuals' personal need for interpersonal skills that made such training necessary. See the next topic, *Wants vs Needs*, for more on this subject.

Wants vs needs

Assessing the need for training is a constant balance between the corporate view and the individual's development ideals. Although there should be a significant overlap (or the trainee is probably in the wrong job), there will always be differences of priority.

Gaps and desires

For a number of years I was a manager of teams of IT people, usually involved in personal computers or the impact of new technology. Conventional wisdom had it that I should concentrate my first year's training budget for new staff members on the technical training they needed for the job. However, I found in practice that I was better making sure that a large proportion of that first year's budget went on interpersonal skills.

The fact is, these were mostly technical people, who would pick up most of the technological requirements without much training. They had a natural feel for what was required. However, they also needed to interact with people to do their job well, and were rarely well equipped in this area. By taking a broader view of the requirement, I made more effective use of the training budget.

At first sight, the balance between corporate and personal needs is a clear one. The business is paying for the training, so business priorities have to dominate. Unfortunately, it's not so clear-cut in practice. Certainly it's true that straightforward operational training has to have top priority, but it's a lot less obvious when, for instance, a member of staff feels that his or her presentation skills need improving while the company would rather he or she had assertiveness training.

Particularly with the soft skills, training needs the trainee's engagement to be effective. If the trainee doesn't feel that the training the company has recommended would be beneficial, the whole exercise will prove a waste of time and money. What is needed is a crossover between the trainee's personal training goals (see *Matching the individual* above) and the company's requirements.

If possible, for each individual, put alongside each other prioritized lists for desired personal and company training. See how many of the highest priority items in both can be accommodated. If you need to whittle away, start with the company's non-operational or soft skills training. Only then eat into the personal priorities.

In practice this does not need to be a big problem. For most people there is sufficient overlap between company and personal goals that many of the training aspirations will be common. However, it isn't enough to assume that this is the case, and undertaking this exercise can make all the difference.

Selling training benefits

If training is to be effective and the training department or company is to be run in a businesslike way, the benefits of undertaking the suggested training have to be sold to a range of stakeholders.

> **If there is one thing I have to spend for ever drumming into new managers it's the need to keep on top of your stakeholders. This involves knowing who they are, exploring their motivations, making sure that they are happy with what they are told and what they are given. If you keep in constant, effective communication with your stakeholders it's hard to go wrong.**

> *A corporate senior manager*

The manager above wasn't specifically talking about training, but the argument applies equally well there, and training is an area where the whole concept of stakeholder analysis may have less penetration than in some aspects of business.

What are stakeholders?

'Stakeholder' is one of those words that gets bandied about so much in business circles that it's easy to assume incorrectly that everyone knows what it means. ('Paradigm' is another such word, but arguably anyone using it is in need of re-education with a large stick.) The simple original meaning is everyone with a stake in an enterprise, but that stake can take many forms. It might mean a financial stake, a political stake, a power stake or a personal stake. In essence, it's anyone who can influence or be influenced by whatever they are stakeholders in.

This can be overextended. You can argue that everyone employed by a company, every shareholder and every customer is a stakeholder in anything the company does – but this is not a particularly valuable definition. It is much better to keep it to the tight group of people who are most affected by, or can have most effect on, the subject.

Who are the training stakeholders?

The principal stakeholders in training are the trainee, the trainee's manager, whoever pays for the training and whoever provides the training. For the purposes of selling it is the first three who count most. Of course it's quite possible that the trainee's manager also pays for the training – or for a small company, the same person may be in all three roles of trainee, manager and custodian of the finances. The important thing is to be aware who the potential stakeholders are for your planned training.

How should we communicate with them?

The usual failing with stakeholders is to keep up a two-way communication. If you are delivering anything, you need to find out what your stakeholders expect, make sure your picture matches theirs, update them with changes and continue to ensure that their requirements haven't changed with time. When you have delivered, you need to be sure that the stakeholders are happy with the results.

One of the most important aspects in dealing with stakeholders is realizing that timeliness needs to be approached from the stakeholders' viewpoints. The temptation is to apply your own sense of timing. You know very well that a particular action isn't particularly important to the stakeholders. It won't make the slightest difference to them whether they hear about it today or next week. But from their viewpoint things can be very different. That delay can seem intolerable. The essence of dealing with stakeholders is getting into the subjective nature of time and communications. It might sound darkly philosophical, but actually it's very practical.

How can we sell training benefits to them?

The first answer to the question 'how can we sell training benefits?' is a question itself – what motivates your stakeholders? What will get them involved? What are they trying to achieve and how can you make your training help them? If you are new to selling, beware of the trap of over-selling. It's very tempting to say that your training can achieve practically anything. If that's what your stakeholder wants, that's what you say the training will deliver. Once you have the stakeholder signed up you will untangle the mess. Unfortunately, good though this approach may be at getting business the first time, it will damage your reputation, and before long no one will trust your assessment of what you can and can't deliver. It's much better, if the requirement is outside your capabilities, to be up front about your limitations, but to say that you can certainly find someone who can deal with this particular aspect.

Finding out what the stakeholders are trying to achieve (and remember we are talking about the potential trainee, the trainee's manager and the person who pays) is a non-trivial task. It means getting a lot of information about your potential trainee and, even worse, it means understanding that information. But unless you can get a grasp of your stakeholders' intentions and what they actually mean, you have little chance of selling effectively.

Once you have that basic analysis, it may well be necessary to redefine what you are offering. Some flexibility is essential (see *Flexible development*, page 146). But then you should have a reasonable picture of what it is that you have a chance of selling. It's a waste of time for everyone if you try to sell something entirely inappropriate, and it will destroy your stakeholders' respect for you. With a targeted set of options you can now move on to illuminate and inspire, giving your stakeholders the picture of what it is you have on offer, and why it is going to be good for them.

Illumination should be very much in the stakeholders' own terms. There's no point telling them that you have a firm grasp on Honey and Mumford's learning styles if they're not trainers. It is jargon that will go over their heads. Make sure that you can answer a series of simple questions:

- What will it cost?
- How long will it take?
- When can we do it?
- What will be different afterwards?
- Will there be any impact on the bottom line?

Inspiration is the part of the selling where you go beyond the stakeholders' basic requirements. Whether or not you are in competition with other training organizations for the job, imagine that you are. How would you differentiate yourself? What makes your particular approach better than the rest? What skills and attributes have you that the competition don't? What special knowledge have you got? What is special about the way you train? Don't hold back from using examples of past experience – other courses you have run. If you can get endorsements from previous customers or stakeholders (and don't be afraid to ask for them if things go well), so much the better.

A final and very important consideration when looking at selling your training is that you should consider real motivations rather than stated motivations. Remember the manager who does the training himself (see page 4). His stated reasons might be that he will get a better idea of what his staff are learning and that it will be a strong force for team building. These are indubitably contributory factors. But he will also be saving money, a driver that will be played down. Similarly, in other circumstances there may be political and other motivations involved. An awareness of these motivations, an ability to look beneath the surface and not take the obvious as truth all the time, is valuable in selling, especially for an internal training department where politics will play a larger part in the decision.

Looking beneath the obvious is a delicate art. It's not a good idea to charge in and say 'I don't believe you when you say this is what it's about. What's your real reason?' That's a great way to lose business. Instead it's a matter of being aware of the psychological indicators – a quick course in body language can be helpful if you aren't already up on it – and also bearing in mind all the realistic, pragmatic reasons that could be underlying the stated position. Is there a way an individual stakeholder can gain from supporting your course? This isn't a matter of embezzlement, but rather of subtle company benefits (like the manager's cost savings) or indirect personal benefit (I can have a good time, it will get my boss off my back, etc).

The most important thing of all in selling training is to remember that that is exactly what you are doing. You are not doing the stakeholders a favour, but selling them a service. Always think 'customer service' as you sell.

Invitations and advertising

Training falls into a group of 'worthy' subjects where there is often reluctance to give a hard sell. Unfortunately, training is in competition with many other demands on budget and time, both fixed resources that can't be stretched forever. It's not a matter of giving training an unnatural gloss, but showing it in its best light.

In the factory we make cosmetics. In the store we sell hope.

Charles Revson

Most of us are suspicious of advertising, especially around a subject as genuinely needed as training. Advertising seems devious, little short of lying to try to get someone to buy something they don't really want with money they can't afford to spend. Yet training is not excluded from the need to advertise and invite effectively. It's not enough to let people know what is happening – you have to sell to them. Otherwise a competing drain on resources is going to elbow you out.

The secret at the heart of good advertising is summed up in the quote above. It is a matter of understanding that the thing you have to sell is not the product alone. It's the way it makes the customer feel. It's the change that the product brings about. It's the experience. In the previous topic we looked at selling the benefits of training. Here we are going to concentrate on some of the less tangible aspects. But don't make the mistake of thinking that this makes them less important. Remember that business decisions are more influenced by gut feel than numbers.

No sell, sell and oversell

The degree of selling in advertising sits on a spectrum from pure fact to pure fantasy. What you are looking for in effective advertising is something in the middle. Having no sell at all – just the name of the course, an outline, training objectives, time, place, cost – is about as exciting as reading a company's mission and goals. Equally, you don't want to so hype the course that the trainees come with totally inaccurate expectations and go away disappointed. But there is something in between.

In advertising and inviting you have three main aims. You have to grab the attention of the potential customers. You have to inform them about some exciting aspects of your product and you have to inspire them to go out and do something about it. Some forms of advertising can also include a mechanism for enabling them to book. The best time to get completion is when the interest is aroused, rather than getting them interested but leaving the booking to another day.

Attention – information – inspiration – execution

You aren't out to shock or irritate your audience like some advertisers, so there are limits to the extent you will go to attract the attention of potential trainees and their stakeholders – but this doesn't mean that you have to be too subtle or retiring. Grabbing attention is a rapid process; you don't have much time. The key attention grabber needs to be an image or a single, short sentence that hits them immediately. For example, an advertisement for a time management seminar might shriek 'THERE IS NO SUCH THING AS TIME MANAGEMENT.'

The aim is to get the audience thinking 'what?' There has to be a sense of intrigue, an encouragement to read more. Compare the line above with a poster or flyer labelled 'Short course in effective time management (unit 17 in a series of seminars on new skills for the management community)'. Your eyes naturally slide off this sort of title, but all too often it's how training is sold.

With the attention grabbed it's time to inform. Give the potential customers a bit more detail. With the exception of adverts that are specifically designed to keep readers entertained in a boring location, for instance on a station platform, the information section needs to be kept to the bare minimum. But this doesn't mean it should be a boring list. The text should flow, picking out the highlights. Let them know up front what your USP (unique selling proposition) is. What are you offering that they don't get elsewhere? This ties into the inspirational details. You don't want the potential customer to be able to answer a quiz on the course, you want them to book it.

Inspiration as far as the customers are concerned is about what the course can do for them, how they will personally benefit (and how their company will benefit) – what they will get out of it and how they will feel. Make sure positive benefits come across strongly without seeming to be exaggerating. Finally, if possible, give them every chance to book right now – phone number, fax, e-mail and Web site, all should be readily available to the potential customer.

Placement

Where you place the advertising and invitations can have a big influence over your results. Creativity in this can make a lot of difference. If the course is internal to a company and simple mail shots aren't getting very far, look at alternatives. Use targeted e-mails as part of the campaign. Use in-house newspapers. Put something on the napkins in the staff canteen or on the seats of meeting rooms. There are plenty of opportunities in the workplace to grab the attention in a different way.

Similarly, external trainers need to go beyond the traditional mass mailing that is obviously training material before you even open the envelope (and often gets dumped in the bin without being opened for this reason). Look for opportunities to reach potential trainees through the editorial side of magazines rather than just advertising (editorial content has more weight with readers). See if a key magazine for your target audience will review one of your training sessions. Use some different aspect of the way you do things to make yourselves news-worthy. (What do you mean, there's nothing different about the way you do things? There will be.) Most of all, look for different, more personal, more targeted ways to reach the people who might be interested in your services. Make sure that includes a good Web site.

Tips of the PR trade

As a journalist I have a constant flow of invitations from public relations firms, all designed to get me to attend an event at which they can push the latest product. The process is more similar to getting people along to a training event than might at first seem to be the case. Over the years, many techniques have been used to get the attention or encourage attendance. Here are a few of the better ones:

● Invitations in the form of a jigsaw puzzle. This has to be used with the right sort of attendee, but invitations that are a challenge can work well.

- Invitations in the form of an audio CD or computer program.
- Invitations using greetings card technology (pop-up or involving card models to build).
- Invitations including a giveaway.
- Incremental invitations. A series of invitations for a single event that start very mysteriously (perhaps a postcard from an unusual location), then gradually add more information until you know what it is.
- An invitation on a mug or coaster or pen. In fact any item that can carry a printed message.
- An invitation that is themed on the subject – eg a security product with the invitation in a padlocked bag.

Some of these approaches are too expensive for a large group of invitees, but it is possible to modify the approach to make it less expensive – for instance, in the last example the security product invitation could have been printed on a padlock-shaped piece of paper. Less impact, but more cost-effective.

Make trainers business people

If you're a self-employed trainer, then you are inevitably running your own business. All to often, though, in large companies the trainers, perhaps unconsciously, exude a sort of academic distaste for the realities of business. This has to change.

> **For me, training requires respect. If I or my managers don't respect the trainer, then the whole effort is without value. The trouble is, all too often they seem to be arts or psychology or (even worse) sociology graduates without a clue about business. For me a great trainer is someone I could throw into a management position without blinking an eyelid. Of course they need skills managers don't have as well, but I want my managers to feel comfortable that a trainer is one of them.**

> *A company director on trainers*

Of course this director has a blinkered viewpoint, but there's an element of truth in there. Respect is crucially important, and whatever the trainers' backgrounds there is bound to be a problem if they aren't familiar with the business environment. Even more so if they have an academic dislike of the hands-dirty aspects of business. One solution is to use a 'real' manager as a trainer (see *Manager as trainer*, page 78). But this isn't always ideal, nor is there necessarily an appropriately skilled manager available. The alternative is to force the business into the trainers.

This has a double benefit. Not only does it increase the respect managers might feel for the trainer, but it also gives a training department or company the ability to apply business skills to the problems the department faces within the company, or the company faces in the competitive world. Whether it's budget, political manoeuvring or publicity, those business skills will prove invaluable.

One approach to cope with this is to increase the number of trainers who are actually running their own businesses. It makes a lot of sense. By bringing in outside staff, the finances can be better controlled – yet where there is a well-established group of small company partnerships, the individuals will still be known and thought of as part of the team.

The small company part here is important. Going to a big training supplier isn't the answer, because once more the trainers don't really need such a feel for business. But where the training is sourced from companies of between one and half a dozen people, they will be close enough to the business coalface to be business people.

Whether you are choosing an external partner or recruiting to the in-house department, you can look for business experience as an important part of the trainer's CV. If the trainer has previously worked in business, been a manager, understands the pressures and realities of business, you have a much better chance of maintaining the respect of those managerial trainees.

Business is a subject where experience counts hugely over training. I'm sorry you've got to hear that as trainers, but it's a fact of life. Many senior managers regard MBAs with a degree of suspicion, because experience has shown that they've got a lot to unlearn before they become effective. It's not that a little management training isn't valuable, especially in the 'soft' skills, but it is not sufficient. If you want to take existing trainers and give them this extra edge, feel free to give them some business training, but do something more. Encourage them to set up their own small businesses, or find them a placement (for at least six months) in line management. It's not easy, it's not quick, but if you want to enhance the business awareness of existing staff rather than recruit or partner with new ones, it is necessary.

Perhaps you aren't involved in training managers and feel this is all a little remote from the realities of your world. There is still a lot to be said for encouraging business skills to ensure that training works in an effective, customer-oriented way. Don't overlook the value of business skills.

Improving an in-house training department's visibility

Trainers are, by their nature, largely self-effacing people. You may get occasional show people in the Tom Peters style of training-as-theatre, but many trainers are more interested in the message than being a star. This is fine, but when the pressure is on, the training department needs to be able to show that it is a powerhouse, capable of changing the performance of the company. It needs to show that its budget makes a significant difference to the bottom line and, most fundamentally, it needs to be seen rather than disappearing into obscurity.

Who?

What in-house training team?

Senior manager of US corporation on being asked to justify bringing in an outside trainer to cover a topic that should have been dealt with by the in-house training team

There's a popular saying in the business world – when the bullets are flying, don't put your head over the parapet. When times are hard in business – and it happens on a regular basis, so we can be sure it will happen again even if things are great right now – there's a feeling that it's better to be hidden than to risk exposure to the bright light of inspection. Unfortunately, this only provides a false sense of security, like a hedgehog rolling into a ball in front of the wheels of a juggernaut. If they are out to get you, it won't matter how low profile you are, you will still be squashed.

Instead of trying to hide, consider the alternative – making yourself so visible that you aren't appropriate for attack. If you really believe that the training you provide makes a fundamental contribution to the effectiveness of the business, you ought to have a story that is worth broadcasting. (If, on the other hand, you think that training is a way to earn a good salary without doing any real work, and it doesn't matter what happens to the business, it's time you found a different job.)

The thing to bear in mind when blowing your own trumpet is that there is an element of competition here. While your aim should not be to do down the IT department and the other service departments clamouring for attention and cash, they are your competitors. Attacking them directly is not a good move – it seems divisive and lacking in company spirit – but it is quite reasonable to be aware of their tactics in selling themselves and to make sure that you top them.

The visibility campaign should run from the ground up. Each time you get a letter thanking a trainer, or complimenting the training, make sure it is percolated up the line, and keep a copy in a big, fat file that is on public view. This approach requires plenty of such letters (a fat file with three letters in it looks pathetic) and a steady flow (when your most recent letter is dated two years ago, you've got problems). If your response is to say 'we don't get such letters', you've a couple of actions to consider. First, make sure what you are delivering is good enough to deserve praise from the trainees. Secondly, ask for them. Don't be shy. If someone says 'that was great', it's quite reasonable to say 'If you really think so, is there any chance of dropping us a note to that effect? It'll help make sure that we can keep up standards.'

Get high-level endorsements too. Try to get people in the organization who are more senior than those who might make the decision to shut you down or trim your budget to say what an essential job you are doing. Look for external endorsement too – from the media and external experts. Even when things are tight, companies don't like being seen to trim back something they've just been praised for in public.

Share your success. When a course goes right, when there is any measurable outcome from a course (quantitative or qualitative), report on it. Let the people who matter (ie those who are going to send other people on your courses and those who foot the bill) know through as many media as possible. If there is an opportunity to get the company good (external) publicity as a result of what you are doing, make the most of it.

The use of external publicity does involve a degree of care, because of the problem we've identified elsewhere – people's motives are not always the ones that they publicly admit to. A while ago I ran a team that was responsible for new technology in a company. As a learning device we put on a fair (see *Fair's fair*, page 41). This was a great success and was covered on national TV news. Not long after, the team was closed down. This doesn't seem to tally with my argument for using external publicity until you realize what happened. Our director appeared on the TV news programme. The deputy director, my boss's boss and the man who closed the team down, did not get a mention even though it was 'his' baby. Big mistake.

And keep things personal. We don't respond well to faceless organizations. We all like to deal with people, and find it much harder to be nasty to known individuals than an amorphous mob. Make sure that stakeholders have specific contacts within your training department or company, and that they get to meet those contacts face-to-face on a regular basis.

ZONE 5

THE AGENDA

This final zone helps the reader build an agenda for transforming training in his or her company, or for his or her staff. It pulls together the message of the previous zones and finishes the book on a practical note.

GETTING THE RIGHT MIX

There is no uniform solution to the training problem. The way that training develops in a particular company is bound to be influenced by a whole host of parameters defining the circumstances and needs at that time. It's for this reason that *Training+* is presented as a mix-and-match set of topics. The important thing is to get the right mix for your particular circumstances.

BUILDING YOUR AGENDA

In the assessment zone (page 15), you were given the opportunity to look at the particular needs you currently face. Now, with an idea of the *Training+* topics under your belt, it's time to pull together an agenda for transforming your training. Look at each of the major sections. Given your priorities from the assessment zone, put together a rough prioritization of the topics. Which are going to give you most impact in the shortest time? Which will have more impact over a longer period? A good agenda for change should combine some short-term results with longer-term work towards major developments.

In putting together an agenda, look for what is possible in the next year, in terms of both time and finances. Make sure that priorities are assessed in terms of both impact on your stakeholders and survival for the training department or company – to do otherwise is to hide reality. And remember that the agenda is not set in stone. Priorities and necessities will change. It is just a starting point.

CREATIVITY FIRST

Arguably the area that most trainers (and most managers) need to launch into most immediately is creativity. It is highlighted in the development action topics (see page 140), but creativity lies at the heart of all enhancements in training, whatever the section. An acceptance that there is something you can do about creativity, and a willingness to take steps to enhance your creativity are essential background to going beyond the theory of *Training+* and making a new approach to training reality. Consider further reading in creativity (see Appendix, page 179).

FIRST STEPS

Review the key topics in each of the five sections of the action zone. Highlight at least one of them that would be of value to you. Pick out at least two more topics that match high priority areas of your need assessment. Look for one that will have very early results, and one that is working to a longer timescale.

With these three topics in mind, put together an outline plan to get some action in place for the topics. Keep it to a single sheet of paper. Don't leave it as a desirable outcome – make sure that action is going to be taken, and that you know by when and by whom. With this in place, you have started down the route to *Training+*. Good luck.

APPENDIX

READING AND RESEARCH

WHERE NEXT

Training+ inevitably covers a wide range of topics beyond the conventional training sphere. The point of this further reading section is not to improve your library on the normal topics of training, but rather to point out new directions that can help build complementary knowledge to aid the training process.

CREATIVITY

Creativity is a subject that is fundamental to the transformation of training. These books will give a background to the nature of business creativity and the practicalities of bringing creativity into the corporate culture:

Paul Birch and Brian Clegg, Imagination Engineering *(FT Prentice Hall, 2000)*
A toolkit for business creativity, providing a practical but enjoyable guide to making creativity work. Introduces a four-stage process for business creativity, equally applicable for a five-minute session or a week concentrating on a single problem. Plenty of depth, but fun too.

Tony and Barry Buzan, The Mind Map Book *(BBC Books, 1993)*
A beautifully illustrated guide to the use of mind maps to take notes,

structure ideas and aid memory. Written by Tony Buzan, the developer
of the mind map concept, with his brother.

Edward de Bono, Serious Creativity *(HarperCollins, 1996)*
A wide-ranging book from the best-known UK creativity guru. De Bono
invented the term 'lateral thinking' and here he explores the benefits of
creativity and describes his personally preferred techniques. Quite a dry
book, but pulls together all de Bono's key work on the subject.

Brian Clegg, Creativity and Innovation for Managers *(Butterworth-
Heinemann, 1999)*
An overview for the busy manager, showing the need for creativity,
where it came from as a management discipline, how it is applied, and
how to make it work in a company. Puts creativity alongside other business techniques, and provides an agenda for introducing corporate innovation.

Brian Clegg and Paul Birch, Instant Creativity *(Kogan Page, 1999)*
This book in the Instants series provides over 70 different techniques for
coming up with new ideas and solving problems, each designed to be
used with the minimum of fuss in an instant.

Roger von Oech, A Whack on the Side of the Head *(Warner Books, 1983)*
In total contrast to de Bono, von Oech's laid-back Californian style
attacks the blockers to creativity in an enjoyable way. It sometimes feels
more like a humour book than a management text, but it is none the
worse for this, and there's a serious message under the gloss.

Tom Peters, The Circle of Innovation *(Hodder & Stoughton, 1998)*
Peters brings his usual bravado to the subject of creativity. Based on the
slides from a series of talks, this book shows Peters' complete return to
form – he is at his best, hectoring the reader on the crucial necessity of
innovation. As the man says, you can't shrink your way to greatness.

SHAREWARE

As described on page 135, shareware is a form of software particularly well suited to supporting your training after the event. You can provide your trainees with a CD-ROM packed with useful products at no cost to the training department or training company. The trainees can try out the software (reinforcing your training as they do so), decide whether to use it, and if so will pay for it themselves.

Finding good, appropriate shareware may take a little time, but is well worth the effort. It used to be that most shareware was either bought from libraries or came on the cover disks of computer magazines. The latter disks are still an effective source occasionally, but generally the best way to home in on appropriate software is using a Web shareware library. It is also worth using a search engine to look for software hosted on its publisher's site.

You will need to try out the different packages to see which, if any, meet your requirements, but it is surprising how often it is possible to provide a handful of products to enhance and support your training.

WARNING – viruses

Viruses are malignant software, designed to do something unexpected, which might range from putting up a silly message to deleting everything on your hard disk. The two main sources of viruses are word-processor documents and programs you run. It is highly unlikely that a piece of shareware from a reputable shareware site like those below will carry a virus, but it is not impossible. Even the biggest names in the software business have occasionally sent out files with viruses attached. If you download either documents or programs from the Web, it is a good idea to have virus checking software on your PC, and to regularly update it, as new viruses appear all the time.

If you are downloading a document, modern word-processor software usually has an option not to run macros (little programs built into the document), which are the only way a virus can be transmitted with a document. Programs can be more sneaky – remember, for example, that not only can the program you buy be infected, but also the setup program that you get to install it.

All the big names in virus checkers have Web sites where you can find out more. See:

- Doctor Solomon (UK but owned by same US company as McAfee) – www.drsolomon.com

- McAfee (US) – www.mcafee.com
- Norton (US) – www.symantec.com
- Sophos (UK) – www.sophos.com

Using a search engine

To use a search engine to find appropriate software, enter keywords matching your requirement, plus *software*. It's probably best not to use *shareware* initially, although you could throw that (or *free*) in later if it is necessary to narrow down the result. So if, for instance, you were running a course on motivating staff, you might use the following search term: *motivation business software*.

Search engines come and go, but if you don't already have favourites, the following might be worth a try. Note: don't stick to UK engines or US engines, try both. It is surprising how often a UK engine might have a different viewpoint, or the bigger US engine might find sources (even if they are UK based) that have evaded the UK engine.

US

- AltaVista – www.altavista.com
- Excite – www.excite.com
- HotBot – www.hotbot.com
- Infoseek – www.infoseek.com
- Lycos – www.lycos.com
- Web Crawler – www.webcrawler.com

UK

- Datagold – www.datagold.com
- Excite – www.excite.co.uk
- Lycos – www.lycos.uk
- UK Plus – ukplus.co.uk

Shareware sites

- Freeware – www.freewareweb.com
- Shareware.com – www.shareware.com
- UK shareware – www.ukshareware.com

TANGENTIAL

Using the Internet effectively is a valuable resource for the trainer, but one that is often left to chance. Internet search skills are only tangential to the training professional in the sense that they are not part of the conventionally recognized skills base. They are still an essential.

Brian Clegg, Mining the Internet *(Kogan Page, 1999)*
The Internet, and particularly the World Wide Web, is a powerful resource for training development, if only you and your clients can find the sources you need. This non-technical book gives readers the skills they need to mine the Internet for information, a crucial requirement for everyone in business in the 21st century.

EXPOSURE WIDENING

These books, of a wide range of types, can be seen as a starting point for opening your mind to different influences (see page 149). They have nothing to do with training – that is the whole point – they are to start widening your inputs to have a more creative outlook.

Jonathan Lynn and Anthony Jay, The Complete Yes Minister *(BBC Books, 1984)*
Along with its sequel, *The Complete Yes Prime Minister*, this superb book from the BBC TV series of the same name captures many of the idiocies of government and bureaucracy to a T. A very funny book, there are lessons for every aspect of business – and plenty of inspiration for trainers too.

Ricardo Semler, Maverick! *(Arrow, 1994)*
One of the best business books ever written. It's not a textbook, but the biography of a company. Despite being located in Brazil during runaway inflation and with potentially difficult unions, Semler took a disgruntled workforce and totally changed their motivation by making their work-place a place they wanted to be. Trust and information replaced traditional management/workforce conflict. It's remarkable.

James Wallace and Jim Erickson, Hard Drive *(John Wiley & Sons, 1992)*
The story of Bill Gates and Microsoft, told without the rosy spectacles of PR. It's a fascinating story and insight into the most outstanding company of the late 20th century. Surprisingly compelling, even if you know little about computing.

Gene Wolfe, Castleview *(NEL, 1992)*
Wolfe is the doyen of fantasists, placing ordinary, slightly inadequate characters in situations that become increasingly separated from reality. It's a wonderful book, and like much science fiction and fantasy beyond the repetitive series books is a great way to turn your thinking in different directions before bringing it back to training.

TRAINING+ RESOURCES

These are training books, but ones that address some particular aspect of relevance to *Training+* – they're training with an edge.

Brian Clegg and Paul Birch, Instant Teamwork *(Kogan Page, 1998)*
Over 70 exercises to help with ice-breaking, warm-ups and timeouts. An essential part of both team building and training, these exercises go beyond the often dull traditional training games.

Margaret Parkin, Tales for Trainers *(Kogan Page, 1998)*
An excellent exploration of the use of storytelling to help learning. Dismissing some of the received wisdom about training, Parkin's book gives a whole new insight into getting the message across.

Reg Revans, The ABC of Action Learning *(Lemos & Crane, 1998)*
More like the YBL of Action Learning, this isn't the easiest read – at times the language verges on the impenetrable – but the concepts are worth exploring, and it is written by the inventor of the concept.

WEB

The Internet, and specifically the World Wide Web, has become an excellent source of information on training. Inevitably a list of Web sites can become out of date before a book is published, but these sites are well worth pursuing:

- Training Zone (UK) – www.trainingzone.co.uk
- HR Guide (US) – http://www.hr-guide.com
- Ideas at Work (US) – http://www.hbsp.harvard.edu/home.html
- International Centre for Distance Learning (UK) – http://www-icdl.open.ac.uk/icdl/index.htm
- Learning Buzz (UK) – http://www.learningbuzz.com
- Learning Matters (US) – http://www.learningmatters.com
- Directory of Mentor Arts (US) – http://www.peer.ca/mentor.html
- Technologies for Training (UK) – http://www.tft.co.uk
- The Biz (UK) – http://www.thebiz.co.uk
- The Training Professional's Gateway (IRL) – http://homepage.tinet.ie/~mjcollins
- The Training Registry (US) – http://www.tregistry.com
- The Training & Development Resource Center (US) – http://www.tcm.com/trdev
- Training Net (US) – http://www.trainingnet.com

INDEX